A Guide to

The UK Publishing Industry

**Paul Richardson and
Graham Taylor**

THE **PUBLISHERS**
ASSOCIATION

ISBN-13 978-0-85386-333-5

© The Publishers Association 2008
First published 2008

Available in downloadable form at:
www.publishers.org.uk

Published by The Publishers Association
29B Montague Street
London WC1B 5BW
Tel: +44 (0)20 7691 9191
Fax: +44 (0)20 7691 9199
Email: mail@publishers.org.uk

Design: Amanda Hawkes
Front cover photograph: © iStockphoto.com/Denis Vorob'yev

Printed and bound in the UK by Lightning Source UK Ltd,
Milton Keynes, Buckinghamshire.

Contents

Preface

The Publishers Association has commissioned this guide to the UK publishing industry for a variety of UK and international readers both within and outside the industry. It is a short work of reference for media journalists and commentators, financial analysts and investors, and policy makers concerned with this very important cultural and commercial sector. It may also be a good starting point for those hoping to pursue a career in publishing either as direct entrants or by studying on university publishing courses. Finally, it should be a useful source of data for overseas publishers approaching the UK market and a basis for further research, even for experienced UK publishing professionals. Those seeking more detail should access The Publishers Association's *United Kingdom Publishing Market Profile* and *UK Book Publishing Industry Statistics Yearbook 2007* on www.publishers.org.uk.

Acknowledgements

The UK publishing industry is now exceptionally well supported in terms of market data – probably more comprehensively than any other publishing market in the world. In this guide we have drawn in particular on data from The Publishers Association Sales Monitor (PASM), Nielsen BookScan and BML (Book Marketing Ltd). We are very grateful to Mandy Knight, Richard Knight and Jo Henry/Steve Bohme respectively for access to their information databases and their exegesis on them. So far as analysis is concerned, not only have we benefited from the views of those industry experts, but from a number of others to whom we are also very grateful. Mandy Knight has also played an invaluable general editorial role in the development of this guide. Additionally we have drawn on a range of published sources, including especially the standard works by Hugh Jones on publishing law and Lynette Owen on rights and contracts, cited in Chapter 6.

Paul Richardson
Graham Taylor

About the Authors

Paul Richardson has worked in and around the publishing industry for 45 years as an author and an editor, marketer, and senior manager in publishing companies including Heinemann, Macmillan, Collins, Octopus and Reed. In 1994 he established the Oxford International Centre for Publishing Studies at Oxford Brookes University and was its Director and Professor of Publishing until 2004. He has undertaken extensive international publishing consultancy, especially in the former Soviet Union, East and Central Europe, and China. In 2007 he wrote The Publishers Association GPI *United Kingdom Publishing Market Profile*.

Graham Taylor is Director of Educational, Academic and Professional Publishing at The Publishers Association. His 35 years in the industry with Heinemann, Collins, Nelson, Longman and the PA have included periods as publishing director, sales director and divisional managing director for both UK and international markets. He is currently Chair of the Publishers Licensing Society, a director of the Copyright Licensing Agency, a trustee of the Publishing Training Centre and sits on several of the key liaison groups that link the industry to other stakeholders in its market.

The Value of the UK Publishing Industries

The Historical Advantage

The introduction of printing with moveable type in the West in the late fifteenth century opened the way to the development of the publishing of books, and later magazines and newspapers, as a major economic and cultural force. The printed word was established as a source of information, education and entertainment, but the social penetration of publishing was relatively slow until the nineteenth century. Thereafter production was transformed by the introduction of steam-powered presses, pioneered in the UK, meeting the needs of a rapidly expanding market for all sorts of printed materials.

In the UK the market was stimulated by the need for a literate workforce in an increasingly urbanised and industrialised society and by people's desire for the self-improvement and enjoyment that the printed word was so good at delivering. Globally it was encouraged by the use of English throughout the British Empire, and by the UK's leadership in international commerce and industrial technology. When the UK's superpower status began to wane in the late nineteenth and early twentieth centuries, the USA increasingly took up that role and assured the continued and increasing importance of **English as the international medium for commerce, culture, science and technology**. This delivered a powerful competitive advantage to the UK publishing industry, which it has been very successful in developing ever since.

The Modern Industry

There are different ways of calculating the total value and scale of the UK publishing media industries, depending on how one treats export sales, income from copyrights, income from overseas subsidiaries and so on, but **in 2007 the domestic publishing market for books, magazines, journals and newspapers was estimated to be worth in excess of £20bn**, representing around 2 per cent of GDP, and employed some 175,000 people. This makes it, in terms of value and employment, somewhat smaller than the telecommunications industries but significantly larger than, say, pharmaceuticals. In the European context, it represents over 20 per cent in terms of value and employment of the publishing media industries in the EU27 as a whole, which in turn account for nearly 30 per cent of the world market by value.

UK publishing media comprises three main sectors, with **books and related forms of publishing representing about 22 per cent of the UK domestic publishing market by revenue**, as against newspapers with 44 per cent, and magazines with 34 per cent. However, it is the fastest growing, and the sector with the largest additional international business.

Although many of the most famous UK imprints were founded in the nineteenth and early twentieth centuries, and a few even earlier, and although some were already establishing international branches before the First World War, **British publishing houses were small to medium-sized enterprises until the 1960s**. Since that time the industry has been transformed with increasing rapidity by concentration of resources, globalisation and technological change.

Now the imprints owned by four major multinational groups, Hachette, Bertelsmann, Pearson and News Corporation, generate over 50 per cent of the sales through the UK total consumer market (TCM). Other international groups have focussed on the educational, academic and professional markets, which are dominated by Pearson, Reed Elsevier, Thomson and others, including the two great university presses, Oxford (OUP) and Cambridge (CUP).

The process of international consolidation continues currently in all sectors. However, there is also constant regeneration with new entrants to the market, especially in consumer publishing – both newcomers and some of the remaining established independents are winning acclaim and prizes for the quality of their publishing and co-operating to make themselves more competitively effective.

The publishing media industries are highly international in terms of ownership and global in terms of operation, especially in the case of book publishing. American, Canadian, German, Dutch, French and Irish corporations have control of leading companies in one or more publishing sectors.

At the same time British-based companies have extensive international publishing interests, notably in the USA, and are world leaders in some sectors such as scientific journals, English language teaching materials, school and higher educational textbooks, children's books and popular illustrated and reference book publishing.

Book and journal publishing in print and electronically differs from newspaper and magazine publishing in a number of significant ways. On the one hand it does not enjoy the massive income stream from advertising that they do. On the other hand it is not threatened by the current loss of that vital income to online channels. It has not suffered from the steady decline in readership that has affected newspapers in recent years, nor the title instability that has affected magazines, with hundreds of closures and launches every year. Book publishing also differs from the other two main sectors in that **it generates an exceptionally high proportion of its revenue in international markets** through the sale of printed books, electronically delivered content and the licensing of publishing rights. **It has also been exceptionally successful in harnessing technology** both operationally and in the creation and delivery of content. In many sectors, such as scientific and professional publishing, electronic delivery is now the norm and of growing importance in all forms of educational and training publishing. So far as consumer publishing is concerned, print is still the norm, but all sorts of new electronic possibilities are rapidly emerging.

● **UK Publishing Media Industries, Revenue* 2001, 2003, 2005, 2007**

	2001 £m	2003 £m	2005 £m	2007 £m	Growth 2001–2007
Newspapers*	7,660	7,755	8,240	8,417	9.9%
Magazines*	5,983	6,014	6,285	6,570	9.8%
Books	3,667	3,858	4,106	4,377	19.4%
Total	17,310	17,627	18,631	19,364	11.9%

* Revenue for newspapers and magazines includes advertising income, conference fees etc.

Source: *Publishing Industry Market Review, May 2006,* Key Note Ltd (www.keynote.co.uk). (Note these figures are calculated on a different basis to those for book publishing produced by The Publishers Association and are useful mainly in terms of comparison)

There are no legal barriers to new entrants, whether companies or individuals, to the publishing media industries, nor controls on foreign investment. They are subject to legislation concerned with intellectual property, monopolies against the public interest, libel and obscenity, but overall the UK publishing industries are amongst the most open in the world both commercially and intellectually.

- **Estimated Value, Market Share and Growth for UK Publishing Media Industries, 2007–10**

	2007		2010		2007–10
	£m	Market share	£m	Market share	Growth
Newspapers*	8,417	43.5%	8,643	41.9%	+2.7%
Magazines*	6,570	33.9%	7,075	34.3%	+7.7%
Books	4,377	22.6%	4,914	23.8%	+12.3%
Total	**19,364**		**20,632**		**+6.5%**

*Revenue for newspapers and magazines includes advertising income, conference fees etc.

Source: *Publishing Industry Market Review, May 2006,* Key Note Ltd (www.keynote.co.uk)
(Note these figures are calculated on a different basis to those for book publishing produced by The Publishers Association and are useful mainly in terms of comparison)

Where is the 'Added Value' of the Publishing Industry?

The UK book and journal industry, once regarded as a rather staid business, is now identified in recent UK government and EC surveys as **one of the most innovative and competitive publishing industries in the world**. In fact, although printing with moveable type came a little later to the UK than France, Germany, Italy or the Netherlands in 1476, historically the UK industry has frequently **led the way in technical and commercial innovation**. It might be said that the UK gave the world many of the basics of modern publishing practice. The **Statute of Anne 1709** is generally recognised as the first legislation to protect the interests of authors and publishers in the Western world and has been regularly updated to take account of technological change and the emergence of new media. The UK was one of the protagonists of the **Berne Convention of 1888**, which provided the basis for the international protection of intellectual property, and today the UK Publishers Association is a leading force in the battle to suppress international copyright piracy. **International Standard Book Numbers (ISBNs)**, which are fundamental to all modern bibliographic and publishing e-commerce systems, had their origins in the UK in 1966 and the UK remains at the leading edge of the development of international standards for the electronic access and delivery of content, bibliographic information and publishing e-commerce. UK book publishers have also been pioneers in the introduction of environmentally friendly strategies for their businesses, for instance in the use of sustainable paper resources and the reduction of chemically damaging production processes.

These very important aspects of publishing may seem rather technical, but beyond them, as subsequent sections of this guide will demonstrate, **UK-based book publishing punches far beyond its weight** relative to its demographic or economic base in terms of creative output and global commercial success. What is also exceptional about book publishing is the multi-faceted contribution it makes to British society in both commercial and non-commercial terms.

The added value of the publishing industry can be identified in at least five main ways. The first is obviously **economic**. This multi-billion pound industry is generally profitable, and in some sectors exceptionally so; it provides high-level and skilled employment; it has attracted considerable foreign direct investment; and it has itself invested strongly in technological change. Around one third of UK publishers' revenue aggregated across all sectors is generated by export sales, worth over £1bn a year, and to these must be added the substantial revenue earned by the licensing of publishing rights, subscriptions to electronically delivered content and the remittance of profits from overseas subsidiaries.

Secondly there is the **educational** contribution. The UK's school, college and higher education systems have relied almost entirely on textbooks and other learning resources supplied by the commercial publishing industry, without the support of subsidies or the 'approved book' systems common to many other societies. UK publishers have competed in their domestic and many international markets through a willingness to work closely with the educational authorities to support their programmes and initiatives, a commitment to the fulfilment of educational aspirations and standards, and by very substantial long term investment in innovation, latterly increasingly in the electronic delivery of educational programmes at all levels. The results are reflected not only in the quality of educational materials available to UK schools and colleges, but also in the extent to which UK-based publishers have been involved in adapting or developing materials for educational systems worldwide. Nowhere is this more apparent than in the global market for the learning of English, dominated by four major and many smaller UK-based ELT (English Language Teaching) publishers.

UK publishers play a major role in the support of the **research, scientific and professional** communities. The first Western academic journals were produced in the UK in the 18th century and today UK publishing is a world leader in the production of STM (Scientific, Technical and Medical) research journals and databases, professional data and training, and business-to-business information. Elsevier's *Science Direct* research database and Oxford University Press's *Oxford Scholarship Online* are just two instances where UK publishers have set new standards in the creation of intellectually rich resources and technically advanced access and delivery. Access to research outputs by scholarly and professional audiences has been significantly extended by the huge investment made by commercial publishers in platforms for the aggregation and delivery of content.

Important as publishing's contribution is to education, scholarship and the dissemination of knowledge, most books are bought for entertainment or the personal enrichment of life. The **social/recreational** role of UK publishing is pervasive. Novels provide not only satisfaction in their own right, but lead on to film and television productions. Cookery, health, travel and history on the television feeds back into more permanent book form. Nowhere is this social contribution more apparent than in children's publishing. That the unparalleled children's publishing success story of recent years, J.K.Rowling's Harry Potter books, originated in the UK might be seen as a happy accident, but UK publishing already had an international lead position in children's fiction, picture books and children's information publishing. UK publishers have also been at the forefront of campaigns to support literacy, reading and the book, not just in terms of the acquisition of essential life skills, but also personal fulfilment. World Book Day, so strongly supported by UK publishers and booksellers, has both supported these goals in the domestic market and raised large amounts of money to provide book aid to the developing world.

Finally there is the **cultural** dimension, hard to define, but no less important for that. It can be argued that UK publishing has given its domestic and international readers a richer and more diverse cultural output than any other publishing industry in the world. Alongside the major commercial publishers in the UK, with a creative output in new publishing which rivals or outstrips that of their American and European competitors, the industry has spawned successful niche publishers for minority groups – feminist, gay and lesbian writing, writing from ethnic minorities and literature in Britain's indigenous Celtic languages – and today much of this writing has also been absorbed into mainstream publishing. British publishers have played a leading part in the development of the international market for work in English from other cultures, such as African, Caribbean and Indian literature, and UK publishing is now increasingly developing its role in opening British minds to translations from other languages. It can be seen as a cultural success for British publishing that in 2007 tens of thousands of Chinese children chose to read *Harry Potter and the Deathly Hallows* for the first time in English, ahead of the release of its Mandarin version, that the UK fiction bestseller list featured an Afghan number one in 2008, or that Arts Council England and Penguin are sponsoring a major programme to improve the quality and availability of literature translations from Chinese into English. These cultural exchanges have a value in their own right, but they also contribute to Britain's 'soft diplomacy', its respect and influence in the world.

PART TWO

The Structure of the Industry and its Markets

Overview of Recent Performance

Summary of Sales Data

The UK domestic market for books and related forms of publishing is **the fifth largest in the world by value** at current exchange rates, behind those of the USA, Germany, Japan and China. These markets are all substantially larger than the UK demographically and in terms of GDP and the UK domestic publishing market has been performing much better in recent years than developed markets of a comparable size to its own such as France and Italy.

The **domestic market** can be measured in various ways. The PA statistics are based on its ***Publishers Association Sales Monitor*** **(PASM)** (www.publishers.org.uk), which surveys participating publishers' sales in terms of value and volume and then grosses the figures up to represent the industry as a whole. In 2007 these amounted to £1.9bn – up 3.4 per cent since 2003, and 498m units – up 12.7 per cent since 2003. The average invoiced price per unit was £3.77 – down by 1.8 per cent since 2003, significantly behind the rate of inflation, which has been running at around 2 per cent a year. To get a value of the market in terms of consumer spending, the PA grosses these figures up to take account of average trade discounts, UK booksellers' exports and the sale of imported foreign books. This calculation suggested a figure of **£3.459bn for 2007**.

Nielsen BookScan (www.nielsenbookscan.co.uk), the leading producer of continuous sales data for the UK and other publishing markets, reported **total retail purchases up from £1.695bn and 225m volumes in 2006 to £1.801bn and 238m volumes in 2007**, increases of 5.9 per cent and 5.6

per cent respectively. The average selling price per book was slightly up at £7.57 in 2007 as against £7.53 in 2006. This is still lower than the average price of £7.60 in 2005, meaning that sales by value have grown by 9.4 per cent and in volume by 9.7 per cent over the two-year period. The comparison with 2005 is a sound one since both years saw the publication of a new Harry Potter, contributing 2 per cent to the market by value.

BML (Book Marketing Ltd) (www.bookmarketing.co.uk), which reports from a long-running longitudinal study of consumers aged between 12 and 79 in the UK, reports sales volumes of 342m units in 2007, up 6 per cent on 2006, and consumer purchases by value of £2.454bn, up 4 per cent on 2006. BML figures suggest an increase in volume of 14 per cent and by value of 11 per cent since 2004. They also report a fall in average prices of 5 per cent in the UK consumer sector since 2004, with more consumer books being bought at a discounted price than at full price for the first time in 2007 (51 per cent discounted, 49 per cent full price).

These surveys are reporting from different bases, hence the variations, but all point to **a strongly performing market**, which has continued to grow despite competition from other sources of information, education and entertainment.

The UK domestic market cannot be fully understood nor the success of UK publishing be properly appreciated without taking into account the industry's **performance in export markets**. These account for **an exceptionally high proportion of the industry's sales** – around 36 per cent of the total by value and 40 per cent by volume in recent years. In 2007 the PASM figures suggest UK publishers invoiced around £1.1bn in exports (up 11.1 per cent on 2006) and sold 356m (up 13.7 per cent). **The UK remained the world's largest exporter of books by value** – somewhat ahead of the USA, whose domestic market is between five and six times as large. Moreover, US exports are heavily concentrated, with 71 per cent destined for Canada and the UK, and 85 per cent going to their top ten markets. UK exports are more diverse, with 59 per cent going to the top ten markets. However, in recent years the rest of Europe has been significantly the most important export region, taking over 40 per cent of the UK's book exports. HM Revenue and Customs figures, which have a rather different basis (including, for instance, exports from British booksellers) suggest that the UK exported £1.5bn books in 2007.

UK publishing can be usefully subdivided into broad market sectors for which the proportions have remained broadly similar in recent years.

- **Market Share of Publishers' Invoiced Sales by Sector and Market, and by Value and Volume, 2007**

Sector	Total		UK Market		Export Markets	
	Value %	Volume%	Value %	Volume %	Value %	Volume %
Consumer	59	73	69	88	42	53
Academic/professional	26	8	21	7	34	10
School/ELT	15	18	10	5	25	37

Due to rounding sum of % may not equal 100%

Source: UK Book Publishing Industry Statistics Yearbook 2007, The Publishers Association 2008.

Creative Output

The UK publishing industry is **one of the most productive in terms of new title output**. Along with the USA and China it produces well over 100,000 new titles a year, substantially ahead of the second tier, which comprises Japan, Germany and Russia, and further ahead of France, Italy and Spain. According to Nielsen BookScan nearly 120,000 new titles were purchased in the UK in 2007 and nearly 760,000 titles published before 2007.

In the past it was possible to monitor this output by the number of International Standard Book Numbers (ISBNs) issued, but this methodology no longer works, because the same titles may have multiple ISBNs for different electronic versions, and a new system of International Standard Text Code (ISTC) has not yet been sufficiently widely adopted to obviate this problem. However, it is clear that the UK publishing industry is a world leader in creative productivity.

The Export of Rights

The international trade in publishing rights is extremely imbalanced. Most developed and developing countries are net importers of intellectual property (IP). Only a handful, led by the USA and followed by the UK, France and Spain, have **a positive balance of trade in book publishing rights**. The UK's largest trade is with the USA, where the balance is, nevertheless, negative, but it has a very substantial positive trade balance in both English-language rights and translation and associated rights worldwide. The value is hard to ascertain. The PA undertook a partial survey of the rights trade in 2004, which recorded rights income of £57m and co-editions income of £71m for 37 respondents. However, the figures were not grossed up and did not take account of income paid directly to authors' agents. An educated estimate suggests the total might have been around £300m. A more comprehensive survey is currently being undertaken.

Trends and Analysis

The Publishers Association statistics, along with complementary figures from Nielsen BookScan and BML, provide an increasingly valuable basis for analysis of longitudinal trends in performance, both in the domestic market and in exports.

● **Publishers' Sales of Books by Volume (net units sold) 2001-07**

Year	Total units (m)	UK Market (m)	Export Markets (m)
2001	729	436	293
2002	723	440	283
2003	719	442	277
2004	758	468	288
2005	788	459	329
2006	786	472	314
2007	855	498	356
% change 2001/07	+17.2%	+14.2%	+21.5%

Source: *UK Book Publishing Industry Statistics Yearbook 2007*, The Publishers Association 2008

● **Publishers' Sales of Books by Value 2001-07**

Year	Total (£m)	UK market (£m)	Export markets (£m)
2001	2,511	1,658	852
2002	2,527	1,674	852
2003	2,591	1,697	894
2004	2,660	1,751	909
2005	2,768	1,768	1,000
2006	2,821	1,817	1,004
2007	2,995	1,880	1,115
% change 2001/07	+19.3%	+13.4%	+31%

Source: *UK Book Publishing Industry Statistics Yearbook 2007*, The Publishers Association 2008

The PA analysis subdivides these total sales into broad categories, as follows:

- *Consumer books* (further divided into fiction hardback and paperback, non-fiction hardback and paperback, reference and children's books)
- *School/ELT* (further divided into school and ELT)
- *Academic/professional* (further divided into: science/technical/medical and social sciences/humanities)

From these figures the PA is able to estimate figures by category for the value of the UK market at ultimate purchaser prices.

● **UK Book Market Categories by Value of Ultimate Customer Purchases, 2007**

Category	UK Publisher Invoiced Sales (£m)	Minus UK Booksellers' Exports (£m)	Customer Purchase of UK Books (£m)	Customer Purchase of Imports (£m)	Total UK Customer Purchase (£m)
Fiction	480	470	893	57	950
Non-fiction	547	536	1,018	65	1,083
Children's	275	270	512	33	545
School/ELT	179	179	241	negligible	241
Academic/ Professional	398	351	493	148	641
Total	1,880	1,806	3,157	302	3,459

Source: *UK Book Publishing Industry Statistics Yearbook 2007*, The Publishers Association 2008

This gives a proportionate breakdown of the UK domestic market by value at the final point of purchase of:

Consumer publishing	74.5 per cent
Fiction	27.4 per cent
Non-fiction/reference	31.3 per cent
Children's	15.8 per cent
School/ELT	7.0 per cent
Academic and professional	18.5 per cent

These figures do not account for scholarly journal publishing and currently the statistics do not generally include e-book or audio-book sales.

The UK Market

UK market continued to grow in volume (+5.5 per cent) and value (+3.4 per cent) in 2007. Children's books rose somewhat in value in a Harry Potter year, and have continued to show the strongest category growth over a five-year period in terms of volume. So far as the UK market is concerned, there are obviously **a number of variables** that affect these results. The first is discounting between publishers, wholesalers and retailers, and the extent to which retailers or direct sales organisations pass on some discount to the ultimate customer. In the UK there is no longer a fixed price for books, but most books have a recommended retail price (RRP), which may or may not be printed on the book. The discounts given by publishers vary according to publishing sector, with higher discounts being given for consumer books, especially mass-market titles, than academic or schoolbooks. They also vary by customer, with wholesalers, chains and supermarkets receiving higher discounts than independent booksellers.

There is also an assumption that the **end customer receives an average discount** on the RRP of 17.3 per cent on consumer books, 11.3 per cent on academic books, and 5.2 per cent on school and ELT titles. These figure hide very large variations: at Christmas time the top sellers may be discounted in some UK outlets by as much as 50 per cent to the consumer, while specialist books are not discounted at all.

Another variable is obviously the average invoiced price of books, which will reflect average discounts and the average RRP. Between 2001 and 2007 in the UK this varied relatively little, hovering around $3.84. Overall, the average price paid by consumers also remained fairly stable at between $7 and $8 again with considerable variations within categories.

A final variation in the figures can be produced by **exceptional sales for one or more titles**. The outstanding example of this in recent years has been the sales of new Harry Potter titles, since these sell in huge numbers in their release in hardback at relatively high RRPs, albeit also heavily discounted. Years in which these titles have appeared, such as 2003, 2005 and 2007, have seen exceptional rises in the proportion of children's books sold and in the average price of children's books in that year. However, over a five-year period the effect is not enough to disguise underlying trends.

The Export Markets

Meanwhile, export sales overall have increased steadily between 2003 and 2007, and the 2007 figure was 11.1 per cent up on 2006. The export picture is a complex one, with variations in performance not only by category, but also by different regional markets. It can be strongly affected by the value of the pound sterling against local currencies. The pound was very strong against the Euro from 1998 to 2003, and then weakened somewhat; it was also strong against currencies in other English-speaking markets such as Australia and New Zealand over the same period, and again has weakened. Against the US dollar it has strengthened steadily since 2001, reaching almost $2.05: £1 by the end of 2007. A strong pound is obviously a barrier to exports in the given markets, especially when UK books are competing with the same title from an American publisher.

In 2007 export sales were up in terms of both volume and value, and have shown strong **sustained growth over a five-year period**. Children's books showed the most growth because of sales of Harry Potter, notably to Europe.

Average export invoiced prices have fluctuated at somewhat over £3 since 2002, but the relationship between volume and value in export markets is a complex one. For instance, there has been considerable increase in the volume export of school and ELT books, but the value has not increased so much because of price resistance in many developing markets.

The performance of individual categories by value has not varied very much in recent years, with academic and professional taking around 34 per cent, school/ELT 25 per cent, adult consumer books 30 per cent, and children's books 12 per cent, though stealing one or two points from other categories in Harry Potter years.

There have been **no tectonic shifts in regional terms** in export sales, but rather gradual growth or erosion of market share, reflecting exchange rates and local economic conditions in the markets. In 2007 Europe represented 41 per cent of exports by value, showing some growth, as did Australasia with 11 per cent, and there was smaller growth in the Middle East and North Africa, with 9 per cent in 2007, and Sub-Saharan Africa with 8.5 per cent. But these broad regional figures hide all sorts of variations country by country.

There are some variations in reporting on export sales figures with PASM, for instance, taking a rather narrower definition of book exports than the Department of Trade and Industry (now Department of Business, Enterprise and Regulatory Reform), which includes maps, booklets and items such as colouring books. The two great rivals in the world book export business, the UK and the USA, also use slightly different definitions. However, it seems to be broadly the case that **since 2003 the UK has maintained a slight lead on the USA**. It is also certainly the case that the UK has a much more broadly based export business in books than the US, which is mainly directed towards Canada, the UK, Mexico and Australia.

● **UK and US Book Exports by Value, 1996 to 2007**

Year	UK	USA	
	£m	**US$m**	**UK£m**
1996	£1,024.2	$1,775.6	£1,136.6
1998	£ 995.6	$1,841.8	£1,112.0
000	£1,017.0	$1,877.0	£1,238.1
2002	£1,051.4	$1,681.2	£1,119.0
2004	£1,035.9	$1,740.5	£ 949.9
2006	£1,100.8	$1,948.1	£1,058.8
2007	£1206.9	$2,135.2	£1,067.6

Sources: The Publishers Association (based on a narrower definition of the Department for Business, Enterprise and Regulatory Reform (BERR) figures) and US Department of Commerce

● UK and US Book Exports by % in Major Markets 2007

UK		USA	
1. Irish Republic	10.7%	1. Canada	45.0%
2. USA	10.6%	2. UK	14.0%
3. Germany	8.6%	3. Australia	5.2%
4. Netherlands	5.0%	4. Mexico	3.7%
5. France	4.4%	5. Japan	3.7%
6. Australia	4.4%	6. Germany	3.6%
7. Spain	4.0%	7. Singapore	2.5%
8. Singapore	3.3%	8. Korea	2.1%
9. Italy	3.1%	9. India	1.9%
10. South Africa	3.0%	10. China	1.4%
Rest of the World	41.2%	Rest of the World	16.9%

Source: Department for Business, Enterprise and Regulatory Reform (BERR) and US Department of Commerce

Where the UK and the US are head-to-head in supplying English-language books to the emerging super economies such as India, Brazil and China, their results are very close, though affected year on year by exchange rates. In some markets such as Brazil and Japan a significant component of US exports are American English learning books published by the US subsidiaries of UK companies such as Pearson and OUP.

Some trends in the figures for both the UK and the USA – for instance, a decline over a ten-year period of sales to Australia and South Africa – can be explained by the increase in local printing by UK and US subsidiary companies in those markets. Another complication is how co-editions are recorded of books originated by UK and US publishers but printed abroad – say in China – and shipped direct to another foreign market. The figures used here are more useful in suggesting trends than as precise statistical measurements.

Usable figures for the country of origin of **UK book imports** are also difficult to establish, since the official figures tend to be a mixture of straight imports from foreign publishers, in which case the USA is overwhelmingly the most important source, and imports of books manufactured for British publishers abroad, in which case the main sources of supply are China, Hong Kong, Singapore, Italy and Spain.

What is clear is that the **UK publishing industry remains, despite exchange variations, highly effective in the export of books globally** and publishers and authors' agents are also generating substantial and **growing income streams through the sale of rights and co-editions**. Added to this is the income generated by UK-based publishers from subscriptions to scholarly journals and to scientific, medical, legal and business databases and related information services, the over-whelming majority of which are now delivered electronically.

The Structure of the Industry

Over recent decades a new structure to the industry has emerged. At the level of the commanding heights, it is **part of a global industry**, dominated by international giants such as News Corporation (USA), Bertelsmann and Holtzbrinck (Germany), Lagardère/Hachette (France), Pearson (UK), Thomson (Canada), and Reed Elsevier (UK/Netherlands). Below that are some other major players, including the two great university publishing houses, Oxford University Press and Cambridge University Press, and then a shifting scene of independents, some flourishing, some struggling, and many being acquired in their turn by larger publishing entities.

Given that little or no investment in physical plant is involved and most production workflow can be outsourced, publishing is a relatively easy industry to enter, especially with the help of information technology. Nielsen BookData has more than 60,000 publishing imprints in the UK and Ireland on their records. That is to say, there are around that number of indi-viduals or organisations that have applied for ISBNs. Altogether 44,135 had UK addresses, and that number included imprints as well as distinct compa-nies. Nielsen reckon there are around 20,000 active publishers and they had 2,900 new applications for ISBN publisher prefixes in 2007. However, fewer than 2,300 publishers were registered for VAT in 2007 (the compulsory VAT threshold for registration being £64,000 sales revenue), and 2,000 of these had revenue of less than £1m. **Only 85 had sales of more than £5m**, and in all the major sectors of publishing over two-thirds of the business was being done by the top ten companies. So, although there are a very large number of small companies, the large, mainly international, media corpora-tions dominate UK publishing after a series of acquisitions and mergers over recent decades.

The number of small publishers remains fairly constant, with those failing or being acquired being replaced by newcomers, but **the number of medium-sized companies has steadily declined**. Overall the number of significant companies has dropped by 10 per cent in the last decade.

The average sales revenue of book publishing companies registered for VAT is £1.5m, and the average number of employees is 13, but these are just numerical averages, and do not reflect the profile of the industry, which is now **polarised increasingly between many small companies employing fewer than ten people and the industry giants**. Of the 2,330 companies registered for VAT, around 1,830 had four or fewer employees, and **just 15 had more than 250 employees**. A handful, such as OUP, Reed Elsevier, Hachette, and Random House, employ 1,000 or more people in the UK.

● **Profile of UK Book-publishing Companies Registered for VAT, 2007**

Sales Revenue		Employees	
£ '000	**Companies**	**Number**	**Companies**
£0–49	805	0–4	1,830
£50–99	400	5–9	240
£100–249	445	10–19	115
£250–499	235	20–49	80
£500–999	155	50–99	30
£1,000–4,999	205	100–249	20
£5,000+	85	250+	15
Total	**2,330**		**2,330**

Source: *UK Business, Activity, Size, Location, 2007*, Office for National Statistics

The Multinationals

In each of the major publishing sectors over half the market by value (and sometimes, as in the case of fiction publishing, 90 per cent) is now controlled by fewer than ten publishing companies. These major international companies, some British-owned and some not, all have publishing operations in the UK but operate internationally, with many of them having their largest sources of revenue in the USA. These publishing businesses have global sales of £1bn up to over £5bn, such as Reed Elsevier, and may be parts of even larger media groups with sales of over £12bn, such as News International.

In **consumer publishing** the UK market is dominated by the imprints of the French-owned Hachette Group with over 16 per cent market share, the Random House Group, ultimately owned by the German media giant Bertelsmann with over 14 per cent, the Penguin Group, owned by UK-based Pearson with over 11 per cent, and HarperCollins, part of the US-based News Corporation with 9.5 per cent. Some way behind these giants come Macmillan, part of the German-owned Holtzbrinck Group, and Simon and Schuster, owned by Viacom of the USA.

In the more specialist **scientific, medical, professional and business markets** there are other multinational giants, including the Anglo-Dutch Reed Elsevier, Canadian-based Thomson, and Dutch Wolters Kluwer. There are other multinationals that specialise in children's publishing such as Scholastic (USA) and Egmont (Denmark) and others again in educational publishing such as Pearson, McGraw Hill and Cengage Learning.

The multinationals have been formed by a process of acquisition, merger, and disposal. Increasingly they have **specialised in one or more sectors of publishing**. Bertelsmann for instance sold off its profitable academic publishing because it was not core business, while Reed Elsevier and Thomson have exited from consumer and educational publishing to focus on high value, mainly electronically delivered, specialist publishing markets.

In recent years the multinationals have continued to buy market share as well as expanding organically. In 2007 for instance the American academic publisher Wiley bought the UK Blackwell publishing business for over £500m, while the BBC's consumer publishing was mostly bought by Random House. Large as they are, even these giants are not themselves immune to takeover, although some are structured in such a way that makes a hostile bid very difficult. But public companies with widely dispersed shareholdings, such as Pearson and Reed Elsevier, are potentially vulnerable. Both have been viewed as possible targets for private equity groups, which would almost certainly break them up and sell off the constituent parts.

The Major Independents

The major independent publishing houses vary from companies that are of large to medium size, with sales revenue of up to £100m, some of which **are strong in a particular sector of publishing** – Bloomsbury (UK publisher of Harry Potter and literary fiction), Quarto (illustrated books), Thames & Hudson (art books) or Faber (a leading literary publisher) – to smaller companies with a turnover of around £500,000. Some are limited companies, some are owned by families or individuals. A few, such as Bloomsbury, are publicly quoted. In some cases (those cited above, for instance) they also have operations in the USA and elsewhere in Europe and Australia.

Although increasingly outsized by the 'big four' trade publishers and the major academic and STM content providers, the substantial independent publishers have a **very important role in UK publishing**. Recently the Independent Alliance, a joint sales and marketing operation for independents headed by Faber and including Profile/Serpent's Tail, Icon, Canongate, Atlantic, Short Books, Portobello and Quercus, has put on impressive growth and would, collectively, rank as the sixth or seventh biggest trade publisher in the UK with turnover of around £40m if it was a combined group. These and other independents have had a notable run of recent successes in winning prestigious prizes and scoring with unexpected bestsellers.

Independent academic publishers, such as Continuum (teacher training and religion), Jessica Kingsley (social sciences) and Berg (history), are serious contenders in specific sub-categories of the market.

The University Presses

The university press sector is **dominated by two large houses** – Oxford University Press (sales revenue over £450m in 2006/7) and Cambridge University Press (sales revenue over £150m in 2006/7), which operate in much the same way as the other international commercial publishers, except that they are departments of their universities and they currently enjoy charitable status and therefore tax advantages in the UK. OUP employs 4,800 people worldwide, including over 1,000 in Oxford. It is not only a major academic publisher, but also the leading UK publisher of dictionaries, one of the world leaders in ELT publishing, and one of the major UK schoolbook publishers. The smaller CUP is also a serious contender in academic, ELT and schools publishing.

Otherwise, the UK university presses are **generally small or very small operations**, with sales revenue of £3m or less per year. The leading presses are Manchester, Liverpool, Edinburgh and the University of Wales Press. Most UK university presses are non profit making by commercial standards, and most are subsidised in various ways by their host universities. Some American university presses, such as Yale and Princeton, also have significant publishing as well as sales presences in the UK.

The Small Independents

There are **thousands of very small publishing operations** run by individuals or co-operatives which publish in specialist areas including poetry, art and regional or local-interest subjects. A number receive quite modest amounts of subsidy from official bodies such as Arts Council England (www.artscouncil.org.uk), the Scottish Arts Council (www.scottisharts.org.uk), Northern Ireland Arts Council (www.arts-council-ni.org) and the Welsh Books Council (www.cllc.org.uk). In Wales, Northern Ireland and Scotland special support is available for publishing in the Welsh, Gaelic and Scots languages as well as English. In commercial terms they are marginal, but they have significant cultural importance in their communities and market niches.

Book Packagers

Book packagers play an important part in the publishing industry, especially **in illustrated non-fiction adult and children's books and reference books**. Packagers may create book proposals with sample materials on their own initiative. They then pre-sell projects to UK, US and other international publishers or retailers wanting own-brand books. Alternatively, they may be commissioned to develop projects by publishers. The relationship allows the publisher or retailer to access a range of creative editorial and design ideas from outside the company and, in effect, freelance the development work of the project. The packager may or may not also manage the printing and make the international co-edition deals, depending on who controls the rights. This works especially well with highly illustrated books and works such as dictionaries and encyclopaedias requiring intensive and specialised editorial work. The Continuum/PA *Directory of Publishing 2008* cited in Part 6 carries a list of packagers, and the market sectors in which they operate.

Other Publishing Organisations

There are a number of other organisations that publish books, journals and electronic material, but do not fall easily into the above categories. The government has privatised most of its publishing, but still publishes the official mapping for the country and supplies commercial publishers with base maps for their own publications through the **Ordnance Survey**. Scholarly organisations such as the Royal Society of Chemistry or the Royal Institute of British Architects are significant publishers in their own fields, especially in the **academic and STM journals** sector. Charities, such as the international aid organisation OXFAM, and religious organisations, may also run their own publishing ventures. Some **professional organisations and companies** in law, medicine and accountancy publish their own materials, as do many training organisations.

Beyond all these are groups and individuals who **self-publish** directly to the public, mainly now via the Internet. Sometimes this form of publishing is an end in itself, or sometimes a way of marketing new and often innovative writing; which, if it attracts popular attention, may later transfer to more traditional forms of publication. At least for the time being, self-publishing remains a peripheral method of publishing. Both authors and readers generally recognise the value that mainstream publishing adds in terms of validation and editorial quality assurance, investment in marketing, sales and promotion, and in accessing diverse channels of distribution.

However, just how the **new opportunities offered by technology** are impacting on publishers and publishing varies enormously by market sector and genre. Each of the major market sectors and the genres within them addresses different readerships: school pupils, students, researchers, professionals, heavy and light readers for pleasure and so on; and different customers: schools, parents, students, libraries, businesses and individuals. They operate through different channels – direct to schools and other institutions, direct supply via book clubs, direct mail and the Internet, mediated by distributors, wholesalers and retailers, both in the UK and internationally. These channels all have different costs and different terms of trade.

So **successful publishing is a complex business**, but one in which UK publishers have shown themselves, so far at least, to be adept at identifying and meeting market demand and in harnessing technology to drive down costs and to improve performance in marketing and disseminating the intellectual properties in which they have invested.

PART THREE

The Market
Sectors

The markets for UK publishers, both in the UK and internationally, can be divided very broadly into three sectors: the school and lower level training market; the academic and professional market; and the consumer or trade market. Each of these broad sectors have their own product needs, scale, structure, terms of trade and channels of distribution and within these broad sectors there are separate genres with further defining characteristics. It is also broadly true that each of them has a different hierarchy of publishing market leaders and each is reacting rather differently to the reality that intellectual property can now be delivered not only in print but in a variety of alternative forms, each with its own costs, and a variety of business models, some now well established, others still being tested.

The School and Training Market

The Structure of Education in the UK

Expenditure on school education and training by the state was £72bn in 2006/7, and this has increased by over 40 per cent since the mid-1990s. At 5.6 per cent of GDP this is about the average for a developed nation, and increases to 6.3 per cent of GDP when private expenditure is taken into account.

In the UK school education is compulsory for children between the ages of five and 16 years. However, 75 per cent of children participate in some form of pre-compulsory education, from the age of three or four years, and 73 per cent of 16-year-olds and 58 per cent of 17-year-olds continue in full time education at school or college. Others combine employment and part-time education or training. The UK has an **exceptionally high proportion of young children coming into education** early in comparison with other developed countries, but **performs less well in retaining pupils after 16 years**. Over 91 per cent of pupils attend free mainstream state-maintained schools; 7 per cent attend private fee-paying independent schools, and around 1 per cent attends special schools for pupils with various forms of disability.

The government has made the improvement in standards of education one of its top priorities, with special emphasis being put on getting all young children off to a good start in life; retaining a higher proportion in education and training after the age of 16 years; seeing at least 50 per cent of young people going on to higher education; and substantially reducing the proportion of adults who lack the skills to flourish in and contribute to a modern society and economy.

The government is now committed to **raising the age for compulsory education to 18** and this is likely to lead to a considerable increase not only in those staying on at school, but also those taking academic and vocational courses in further education colleges.

The School Publishing Market

The precise scale of spending on books, software and other learning resources is hard to determine because of the lack of comprehensive and accurate statistical returns from schools and the variety of channels of distribution. A recent estimate suggests the figures below.

● **UK Market for Educational Books and Software, 2006 £m**

	Core Market	School Library	School Library Services*	Software	Total
Likely (£m)	180	33.3	10.8	60	284.1
Maximum (£m)	218.7	38.1	10.8	65	332.6

* Provision for schools via local libraries, LISU (www.lboro.ac.uk.uk/departments/dis/lisu/index).

Source: *Educational Market Statistics – EPC AGM Statistics Handout 2007,* The Publishers Association 2007

Additionally, about £43.6m a year is spent in the retail market, especially on revision aids for public tests and examinations and 'A' Level textbooks. The revision market is now increasingly also supported by online materials.

The PASM figures for the value of publishers' invoiced sales of educational resources (including ELT) in the UK suggest sales of £179m, a decrease of 16.7 per cent by volume and 1.3 per cent in value since 2003.

Spending by schools on resources overall has increased at about 5 per cent a year since the mid-1990s, but on the whole this has not been reflected in educational publishers' sales. It is thought that the extra money has largely gone into ICT resources.

Schools can set their own budgets, and **there are no government directions on what should be spent on learning materials**. The only direct impact by government on the markets comes when there is a specially funded initiative, such as the National Year of Reading. Indirectly, the market is stimulated when there are changes in the National Curriculum, as there will be in 2008, or in public examination requirements.

Research continues to suggest that parents, teachers and pupils generally agree with the publishers' contention that **spending on learning resources is too low**. There are considerable variations from school to school, and also between the constituent parts of the UK, with spending in Scotland and Northern Ireland higher than in England and Wales. It is also substantially higher in the independent sector.

There is a similar situation with school libraries; again funding for books has been badly squeezed in recent years, but spending is significantly higher in Northern Ireland and in the independent sector.

The market for learning resources has been supplied, very successfully, by commercial publishers, without the potential advantages of approved book systems or the subsidisation of schoolbooks that apply in many other educational systems. They have been required to make substantial long-term investment in materials development in line with curriculum needs, marketing, in-service training and the development of electronic delivery.

The UK educational system was an **early adopter of ICT**, and expenditure on hardware and software continues to be higher than that in most other developed markets. There are over 2m computers, including laptops, in UK schools, and over 250,000 interactive whiteboards and 225,000 digital data projectors. Overall, budgets for ICT were £550m in 2005/06 and £587m for 2006/07. Over and above this the government introduced e-Learning Credits (e-LCs) in 2002, and has extended them to at least 2007/08. These are ring-fenced funds for digital content not hardware.

The Educational Publishers

As in most other sectors, recent decades have seen a **consolidation of educational publishing**. Historically, educational publishing has been a relatively high-margin business, but requiring heavy long-term investment in content development, marketing and, latterly, in electronic delivery of content. Margins have been squeezed, and some of the multinationals, such as Wolters Kluwer and Reed Elsevier, have exited from a market in which they do not perceive a very great growth potential to focus on their other, higher-margin, digitally based information businesses.

A few international companies dominate the field. Pearson, the market leader back in the 1960s and 1970s under its Longman imprint, has regained the number one position in the UK in 2007 by buying its great rival, Harcourt's school business outside the USA and its international testing and assessment business, from Reed Elsevier. Pearson was already the largest educational publisher in the USA and is now the largest worldwide. Wolters Kluwer sold its Europe-wide educational businesses, including leading UK supplier Nelson Thornes, to private equity company Bridgepoint for similar reasons. The other main players in the UK market are Oxford University Press, Cambridge University Press, Hodder Education (Hachette) and Collins Education (News Corporation). There are a number of much smaller operations that specialise in areas such as remedial reading and teachers' books.

In the test and examination revision market, directed at parent purchase through bookshops and on-line delivery, there are two major players – Lonsdale/Letts, part of the Huveaux Group, and the Co-ordination Group – along with the BBC. The main textbook publishers, especially Pearson, also have a substantial stake.

The publishers distribute a large proportion of school learning resources directly to schools. This is supplemented by the educational suppliers, and some sales through bookshops, both to schools and to parents.

Vocational training materials are inevitably more diffuse than those for the mainstream curriculum. These courses frequently mix practical work with self-instruction and assessment software packages and other college-based training materials. This makes it a more difficult sector for publishers, but there are a number of specialists as well as the major educational imprints involved in the market.

The ELT Market

Alongside the school and lower college markets for curriculum textbooks, educational software and other learning materials, there is also a very important UK and export market in English Language Teaching (ELT) materials. Four leading UK publishing houses are among the world leaders in the English Language Teaching (ELT) market: Pearson, OUP, CUP, and Macmillan. The first three of these publishing houses also have American subsidiaries and publish American English materials especially for markets in Latin America and Japan. Macmillan also publish American ELT, but from the UK. For them, and for the smaller UK-based ELT publishers, export markets provide the bulk of their income. However, 600,000 foreign students come to the UK each year for short courses, or full years of study, and there is a domestic market worth around £16m at publishers' invoice value, or £24m at retail value.

The International Trade in School and ELT Materials

In 2007, school and ELT books represented **37 per cent of all book exports by volume**, and 25 per cent by value. This is slightly down on the market share in 2006, but over a five-year period represents an increase. Europe is by far the largest market by value for exports (48 per cent), mainly for ELT books, followed by East and South East Asia (15 per cent), Latin America (14 per cent), and Sub-Saharan Africa remains at 8 per cent: the market is mainly for schoolbooks, and is strongly affected by the availability of international aid programmes for books. This is a field in which Macmillan, which has largely withdrawn from the UK educational market, is especially strong along with the other leading textbook publishers.

There is a growing market for licensed material and joint ventures, notably for ELT materials in China and elsewhere in Asia.

The Academic and Professional Markets

The Structure of Higher Education

There are around 170 institutions of higher education in the UK, educating 2.3m undergraduate and postgraduate students. About 4 per cent of these come from elsewhere in Europe, and 9 per cent from the rest of the world. **Student numbers have risen dramatically** since the 1960s, from fewer than 500,000, and are set to continue to increase as the government aims to get 50 per cent of young people into higher education. There are 160,000 full- and part-time academic staff, about 25 per cent of whom are engaged purely in teaching and 25 per cent purely in research.

Undergraduate students contribute to their fees, and most postgraduates pay the full cost of their fees, although at doctoral level they may get research funding. The higher education sector receives around £18bn annual income, of which just under 40 per cent comes from the government funding councils, 24 per cent from student fees, and 16 per cent research grants.

For details of all aspects of higher education there are a number of websites, notably www.hero.ac.uk – a comprehensive higher education portal – and www.UniversitiesUK.ac.uk.

There is additionally a substantial market for those engaged in continuing professional development outside the higher education system.

The Higher Education Publishing Market

UK publishers' invoiced sales into the higher education publishing market were worth just under £400m in 2007. Allowing for the substantial importation of academic and professional books, the estimated retail value of the market was £641m. To this must be added the very substantial sale of academic journals and other digital products. The market divides between academic textbooks, monographs, journals and other digital products, the latter three being mainly for libraries.

Undergraduates on full –time curses spend around £120-£130 per year book books, and postgraduates closer to £400. Total undergraduate expenditure was approximately £220m in 2006/07. Students and lecturers continue to place a high value on textbooks, but students are increasingly burdened with debt and have a range of choices apart from buying a new textbook. These include **a growing second-hand market**, course packs, and virtual learning environments (content on university intranets and the Internet itself). Academic publishers have collectively launched a project to promote the academic textbook: 'Open Books, Open Minds' (www.openbooksopenminds.co.uk).

Monograph publishing is especially important for academics in the arts and humanities, and to a lesser extent the social sciences. It is a challenging area for publishing, given the pressure on library budgets on the one hand and the growing number of academics seeking publication to raise their research profile on the other hand. Print-on-demand (P-o-D) and other forms of electronic access may offer a partial solution to the problem, but new publishing models still need to be worked through.

Legal and Medical Publishing

Legal and medical publishing extend beyond academic study and research into **valuable professional, commercial and industrial markets**. These have proved to be especially appropriate for electronic publishing and, given the high margins that can be achieved and their global markets, they have attracted major international groups such as Reed Elsevier, Thomson, and Wolters Kluwer that are at the cutting edge of delivering digital content.

Academic and Specialist Libraries

There are around 850 academic and research libraries in the UK. They spent £187m on information provision in 2005/06. Of that 55 per cent was spent on journals, 17 per cent on other electronic products and 28 per cent on books. However, expenditure on journals has risen steadily over recent years, and expenditure on other electronic products has risen significantly, while expenditure on books has been static or falling.

Academic libraries rely mainly on specialist suppliers such as Blackwell or Coutts for books, and subscription agents for their journals. The Joint Information Systems Committee (JISC) (www.jisc.ac.uk) has developed model site licences for electronic versions of journals for libraries.

Journal Publishing

Academic journal publishing, especially in the scientific, technical and medical (STM) sector, is **a very large global business**, worth up to £7bn a year at purchase price. UK journal publishers have up to one-third of this market. Probably 75 per cent of their sales are in export markets, but that still leaves a substantial domestic sale. This has become a contentious area of publishing. On the one hand it is dominated by large publishing organisations, led by Reed Elsevier with over 2,000 journals, followed by Springer, Wiley-Blackwell, Thomson, Kluwer, and Taylor & Francis, for whom this is a profitable business. On the other hand, there is a powerful movement, known as **Open Access**, led by a community of funders, academics and librarians who argue that publicly funded research should be freely accessible electronically to the academic and public communities. There are complex issues concerning the funding for publication of research outputs and the value added by publishers. There is a balance to be struck between the legitimate business interests of publishers and the access needs of research and other communities, especially in the developing world.

Electronic Publishing

The majority of journals are delivered electronically, but electronic publishing is also extending into many other areas of academic publishing. Publishers themselves, such as OUP with its *Oxford Scholarship Online* programme, have begun to build up their own databases of content which can be accessed and customised by users. There are also a number of aggregators, mainly selling or licensing access to academic libraries.

A number of **political and legal issues** arise from electronic publishing.

These include the tension between the desire of national governments and the EC to make research and other data more widely available electronically, and the desire to support important commercial interests. There is also tension between some libraries and providers of digital information and services such as Google on the one hand, and publishers, authors and others concerned to uphold intellectual property rights on the other hand. These issues surface around initiatives such as the EC's programme for a **European Digital Library**.

Lifelong Learning, Professional Development and Distance Learning

The UK government is strongly committed to the encouragement of lifelong learning and professional development to maintain a highly skilled and flexible workforce trained to meet the requirements of a modern economy. This includes offering training to low-skilled adults, and encouraging those working in declining industrial sectors to retrain. This is largely the responsibility of the Learning and Skills Council (LSC) (www.lsc.org.uk), which will be disbanded in 2010 in favour of the local authorities and a new Skills Funding Agency, and the regional economic development agencies. At the other end of the scale there are major publishing opportunities associated with the delivery of higher professional qualifications.

All these forms of training are delivered face-to-face in colleges, and by commercial training organisations. They are also areas where open and distance learning is especially appropriate.

The Academic and Professional Publishers

The market divides into distinct sectors. The higher education textbook market is led by Pearson and other large international groups such as McGraw Hill, Cengage Learning (formerly part of Thomson), Sage, Taylor & Francis, and Wiley. The scientific research and specialist market is led by Elsevier, along with Springer, Wiley-Blackwell, Taylor & Francis, Thomson and Wolters Kluwer.

In the arts and humanities, for both journals and monographs, the market is more fragmented, and a number of smaller publishers have established niches alongside major international academic publishers such as OUP.

Training materials may be delivered by colleges and training organisations, increasingly online, by professional organisations themselves, such as the Royal Institute of British Architects, or a quite diverse range of commercial publishers, including both the large groups and small specialists.

Academic books are sold through **high street and campus bookshops**. There are some chains such as Blackwell and John Smith that specialise in this sector, and also specialist medical and legal bookshops such as Hammicks. Increasingly the trade is migrating to the Internet, with publishers themselves, academic booksellers, specialist academic websites and Amazon offering e-retailing, and content being delivered digitally for downloading. There is also a growing second-hand market operated both by individuals and commercial operations.

The supply of books to academic libraries is largely handled by specialist library suppliers and journals by subscription agents.

The International Trade in Academic and Professional Publishing

Academic publishing, especially in the STM sector, is essentially a global business. Arts and humanities and professional publishing tend to be more market-based, but still have some international sales. **Academic and professional publishing accounts for over one-third of the UK's book exports by value.**

Over half the UK's academic and professional book sales by volume, and 48 per cent by value, go to export markets. The majority of journal subscriptions are from overseas customers. Over and above this there is considerable licence income for territorial and translation rights.

At the same time, the UK is a very strong market for foreign academic product, especially from the USA. A number of major American commercial and university presses have full publishing operations or sales and marketing offices in the UK, and many more have local sales representation and distribution arrangements. **About half the books imported into the UK, by value, are in this sector.**

The Consumer Market

In the UK domestic market, according to the PA survey in 2007, consumer books accounted for 88 per cent of published invoiced sales by volume, and 69 per cent by value – proportions that have been fairly constant over the last five years. Consumer books can most usefully be subdivided into **adult fiction**, which accounted for 33 per cent by volume and 26 per cent by value; **adult non-fiction and reference**, which accounted for 25 per cent and 29 per cent respectively, and **children's books**, which accounted for 25 per cent by volume and 15 per cent by value. These ratios have also been fairly constant, but with children's books taking an extra 1 per cent or so in the years when a new Harry Potter was released.

Average invoiced prices decline in 2007 for fiction by 2.7 per cent to £2.95, and for adult non-fiction by 2.5 percent to £4.34. The average price for children's books rose 12 per cent to £1.82 in the year of a new hardback Harry Potter.

In terms of volume sales, the 2007 bestseller lists were dominated by fiction, with the adult edition of Harry Potter at number one followed by a number of literary and mass-market novels. A number of media tie-in or celebrity autobiographies also sold very strongly along with some novelty titles. Several relatively unknown novelists were represented there, largely due to their exposure on television through the Richard and Judy book show.

The major international publishing groups have increasingly dominated the consumer market in recent years, with the market leaders increasing their market share by both organic growth and acquisition. The 'big four' groups – Hachette, Bertelsmann, Pearson, and News Corporation – took over 50 per cent of the Nielsen BookScan's TCM by value in 2007, and the process of acquisition by these and the smaller groups is continuing into 2008.

Fiction

In 2007 fiction sales were up by volume and value. The genre is dominated by the large groups, with the **'big four' taking 85 per cent of the market by value**, and the top ten companies taking over 95 per cent. However, independent publishers Bloomsbury, Faber, and Canongate all made it into the top ten, and **the independents once again performed well** in terms of critical acclaim and literary prizes.

Fiction as a genre is characterised by large royalty advances, not only for established bestselling authors, but also exceptional newcomers. There is also a high spend on marketing, and heavy discounting, both from the publishers to the retailers, and by the retailers on to the consumers. Fiction titles may have several lives as hardbacks and in various paperback forms, but the bestselling lists are dominated by new titles.

Adult Non-Fiction

The 'big four' also have a quite powerful position in the adult non-fiction sector, taking 47 per cent of the market by value in 2007. But this is **a much more diverse market**, with the top ten publishers accounting for around 58 per cent, and many smaller companies sharing the remaining 42 per cent.

Within certain sub-categories of the market, such as travel, specialist publishers have been able to challenge the big groups.

Some kinds of non-fiction, such as celebrity autobiographies and media tie-in titles, behave like fiction titles with large advances, heavy marketing and discounting, and a relatively short shelf life, but others, such as dictionaries, popular reference books, and travel guides may have a long selling life, and are less likely to be discounted.

While with fiction the great majority of titles are acquired through authors' agents, who may retain many subsidiary rights for the author, in some areas of non-fiction **the more common pattern is for publishers to commission the product**, and in this case they may well have full publishing rights. Illustrated non-fiction publishers may also contract out the product development to packagers, or buy concepts for development from them, and be in a position to benefit from the international co-edition business.

Children's Books

The profile of the children's market is rather different again, with the **'big four' being strongly challenged** by publishers such as Scholastic, Egmont, and Walker that specialise in children's publishing. In recent years Bloomsbury has challenged Penguin (Pearson) for the top spot in a year when a new **Harry Potter** has been released, but is not in the top ten in other years.

Quite apart from J.K. Rowling, there are very popular children's novelists who generally lead the bestseller lists, such as Philip Pullman, Jacqueline Wilson, and Anthony Horowitz, and their titles tend to have a longer shelf life than adult bestsellers. Modern children's classic picture and storybooks may continue to sell strongly for decades. Moreover, books based on popular children's characters such as Thomas the Tank Engine and Winnie the Pooh can generate massive additional income flows from media tie-ins and character merchandise. Others are themselves spin-offs from children's television or films.

Overall the UK children's sector, although disadvantaged by relatively low retail prices, has **performed very strongly in recent years**, despite competition from other media. BML figures for the UK market suggest that children's publishing has grown by 18 per cent by volume and 29 per cent by value over the last four years, well ahead of adult consumer publishing. If Harry Potter sales are not included the growth has still been 11 per cent by volume and 14 per cent by value.

Audio Publishing

Audio publishing was until quite recently a relatively low-key sector of the consumer publishing business, but it has been **boosted by technological change**, although market penetration is well below that achieved in the USA. CDs have now almost entirely replaced audiocassettes, and it seems that increasingly the growth in the market will come from downloads or other sorts of electronic delivery. The market is estimated to be worth around £70m at consumer prices, shared between the large trade publishers, the BBC, and a number of specialists, such as Naxos.

About 30 per cent of the market by value is children's product, followed by fiction, humour, and popular business and self-improvement titles. With the changes in technology there has been a **strong trend towards full text recordings**, and publishers are increasingly using celebrity actors as readers. Audio books are now also attracting serious reviews in the literary pages.

Sales are still quite modest, with even *The Da Vinci Code* apparently selling around 100,000 copies, and 10,000 being a good sale for most titles. However, the market in the USA has seen very rapid growth, and downloading may boost sales in the UK as it becomes more popular. The downside is, of course, that this sort of publishing is more vulnerable to piracy or unauthorised copying.

Electronic Publishing

While the market for electronic product in the STM and business-to-business sectors has advanced strongly in recent years, the progress of **digital technology in the consumer market has been more uncertain**. Early experiments with software for use in the home in the 1980s fizzled out, and a number of publishers suffered costly failures with the launch of consumer CDROMs.

In 2007, however, there were signs of **consumer publishers readdressing the opportunities** in electronic delivery. A number of the large groups have begun to build electronic warehouses of current titles for downloading, and offer a browsing facility on their websites. Publishers are also becoming more proactive in selling direct to consumers off their websites.

Travel publishers, faced with losing market share to free map and guide content on the Internet, have been developing various models for the licensing or downloading of their material or the enhancement of print products via their websites.

There are a number of big issues in this market. First, there is **still not a really satisfactory and affordable reader** to provide the equivalent of the iPod; second, there is the problem that consumers of so much information are used to getting it free; and third, there is **the threat of piracy** or unauthorised copying. At the time of writing Amazon's Kindle reader or Sony's equivalent have yet to be launched in the UK and the new Readius combined e-reader and mobile phone is about to be unveiled, but there seems to be a perception that the iPod moment has not yet arrived – but that it will.

Over the last decade most genres that would seem to be vulnerable in printed form, such as travel and popular reference books, have shown a strong increase in sales, but in the last two or three years that trend has slowed down or even reversed, perhaps with the rapid growth of access to broadband. The market situation is extremely hard to predict, but all the big consumer publishers now have senior strategists working on it.

Public Libraries

The UK public library system has been one of the best developed in the world, with one outlet to every 13,000 people, and a wide range of books for free loan or reference, and increasingly audio and video material, usually charged for, as well as Internet access and other IT services.

However, **the system is now in considerable difficulty**. Although funding has grown in recent years, the increase has gone into staffing, premises, and administration, and **spending on book acquisitions has fallen**, accounting now for less than 9 per cent of the total library budget. In 2006/07, £77m was spent on books, down 0.6 per cent on the previous year and with a predicted further reduction of 1.2 per cent for 2007/08, continuing a ten-year trend. Northern Ireland is the only part of the UK that has seen sustained spending on books for libraries. In recent years there has been a steady increase in expenditure on audio-video materials and computer services, but this too is predicted to flatten out.

As the stock of new titles has become more restricted, so readers have tended to turn to purchase rather than borrowing, although public libraries remain very popular with children, who account for 30 per cent of loans. Local authority library budgets have come under increasing pressure and there have been a number of closures, with more expected in 2008.

The Department for Culture, Media and Sport is working on **a new strategy for libraries** through the Museums, Libraries and Archives Council (www.mla.gov.uk). It especially sees a community role for libraries as centres of activity and learning for children. But some pessimistic commentators foresee the end of adult libraries in the next ten to 15 years. This would be a blow to publishers, for whom the libraries have been a valuable market, especially for fiction. It will also be a loss for authors who may earn a modest income stream from the Public Lending Right (PLR) (www.plr.uk.com), under which each loan generates a micro-payment, amounting to nearly £7m paid to 24,000 authors in 2006/7. There the current maximum payment of £6,600 was paid to 262 authors and there have been protests from author organisations that the budget is not due to increase in the next three years.

Book Retailing

The book trade in the UK has been **transformed in recent decades**. For most of the twentieth century it was dominated by small, usually local, chains and independent booksellers, with just one major English chain, W.H. Smith, and one Scottish one, John Menzies (subsequently absorbed by W.H. Smith). This situation was supported, in part, by the Net Book Agreement (NBA) – a trade arrangement that meant that the publisher fixed the retail price of most books. This discouraged dynamic retail competition. Since the 1990s, and following the collapse of the NBA, the book wholesaling and retailing markets have become increasingly consolidated and competitive.

On the one hand, high-street retailing has consolidated more and more into a small number of national chains – W.H.Smith, Waterstone's, Borders – offering an increasingly wide range of books and competing fiercely in terms of discounts to the customer and other marketing offers. The major chains have also begun to move out of town into the shopping centres. On the other hand, the market has also seen new entrants from the supermarkets and the e-retailers. So the independent booksellers have been in steady retreat, forced out of prime locations by rent increases, but **books have become available through an increasingly varied and accessible range of channels** from garden centres to Starbucks. In 2007 there were some signs of resurgence for the independent booksellers both because of collaborative action between themselves and because the major publishers have come to recognize their importance especially at the top end of the market. However, in terms of market share the chains, the internet retailers and the supermarkets are clearly the dominant channels for books, especially in the mass market for consumer books.

The small bookselling outlets tend to have larger sales than the very small publishers, but also to employ fewer people. At the same time, the large booksellers employ more people than many large publishers. W.H. Smith, for instance, employs over 23,000 people across its whole business. Before the acquisition of Ottakar's in 2006, Waterstone's employed over 2,600 people, and Ottakar's over 2,000. Part of the rationale for the merger was the staff reduction that would be possible, especially in back-office functions. Borders employs over 1,500 people and Blackwell around 800. At the other end of the scale, the great majority of bookselling companies employ fewer than ten people. In 2003 there were 6,765 bookselling companies registered for VAT. In 2007 that was down to 5,310.

● **Profile of UK Bookselling Companies Registered for VAT, 2007**

Sales Revenue		Employees	
£ '000	Companies	Number	Companies
£0–49	710	0–4	3,540
£50–99	925	5–9	1,235
£100–249	1,585	10–19	365
£250–499	1,190	20–49	115
£500–999	590	50–99	25
£1,000–4,999	260	100–249	10
£5,000+	50	250+	20
Total	**5,310**		**5,310**

Source: Office for National Statistics, UK Business, Activity, Size, and Location, 2007

At the same time the **e-retailers**, notably Amazon, **have also grown rapidly**, and the book clubs and the remainder and bargain bookshops have lost share in the face of aggressive discounting in the mainstream bookselling market.

BML figures suggest that sales through chain bookstores have fallen by both volume and value by 4 per cent over the last four years, while sales through the Internet and supermarkets have doubled. BML figures estimate that Internet selling accounted for 21 per cent of the consumer market in 2007. Figures from an HSBC review of book retailing suggest that Waterstone's have 20 per cent of the market followed amongst the chains by W.H.Smith with 13 per cent and Borders with 8 per cent. They estimate that supermarkets account for 10 per cent, half of which was through Tesco, and that Amazon now have 16 per cent with other e-retailers accounting for 5 percent and book clubs and other direct sales 10 per cent.

The Supply Chain

In the past, the majority of publishers handled their own distribution, but increasingly this is only the case for the largest and some of the smallest. Distribution for many publishers is now undertaken either by large publishers who handle other publishers' distribution as a business, such as Macmillan or Hachette, or by stand-alone distribution companies, such as Marston Book Services. Both types of business are able to take advantage of **economies of scale** in terms of transport costs, computer systems and automated warehouses.

There has also been consolidation in the wholesaling and library supply business. There are still a number of regional wholesalers and specialists who handle certain genres of books, but a large part of the business is now in the hands of a few major companies, led by Woolworths, following their takeover of Bertrams in 2007, and Gardners who are competing both for the intermediary role between publishers and smaller retail outlets, and for the mass supply to supermarkets.

With the growing size and power of the key retail outlets, publishers have been under considerable pressure to improve their terms of trade in relation both to retail and wholesale discounts and payment periods. The independents have found themselves increasingly disadvantaged, sometimes finding that they could buy stock more cheaply from a supermarket than from the publisher. Latterly publishers have come to recognise **the ongoing importance of the independents** to the health of the business, and have been looking at ways of giving them improved terms.

With **margins under extreme pressure** in this highly competitive environment, all parts of the book trade have been looking at ways of working together to take costs out of the supply chain. Publishers, booksellers, and librarians have been working collectively through Book Industry Communication (BIC) (www.bic.org.uk) to establish standard information systems throughout the market and internationally. This has been the prelude to the introduction of **e-commerce** throughout the book trade, with a target implementation date for basic systems of May 2008. As part of that process it is also the intention to have the processing of the great majority of returns – one of the most wasteful parts of the supply chain – automated by then.

Meanwhile, publishers and booksellers are looking to improve their performance and cut costs with integrated systems from book trade solution specialists such as VISTA and IBS Bookmaster, and to control their stocks and inform their business systems with the help of continuous sales data such as Nielsen BookScan's. Overall, the efficiency and speed of the supply chain has improved very substantially in recent years. One downside for publishers, however, is that booksellers are able to apply much tighter controls on their stockholding, and rely on just-in-time reordering.

However, there has also been a growing debate as to what the role of the retail intermediary is going to be in the age of e-books, downloads, print-on-demand and publishers selling direct from their websites. This has been the subject of a number of discussion documents produced by the Booksellers Association, which can be viewed on their website (www.booksellers.org.uk).

Consumer Marketing

Another outcome of the competitive environment has been the increasing emphasis put on marketing and the increasing cost of building bestsellers. Publishers broadly divide their activities between marketing to the book trade and marketing to the consumer, but part of convincing the book trade to stock new titles in quantity is by demonstrating the extent of their consumer promotions. Before the demise of the Net Book Agreement, book retailers spent very little on marketing. In the new competitive environment W.H.Smith spent £6m on book advertising in 2007 and Waterstone's over £3m. The supermarkets and book clubs are also heavy spenders on book promotion. Amongst the publishers, the Random House group spent over £3.5m, the Hachette group over £2m. The chains increasingly also expect publishers to contribute to the cost of bookshop promotions, displays, and special catalogues at Christmas and other peak selling campaigns, such as Back-to-School.

Another increasingly important joint promotion is **World Book Day** (www.worldbookday.com), at the heart of which are a small number of special £1 children's books and the distribution of book vouchers to primary school children.

For trade books, reviews, editorial coverage in the media, television and radio appearances by authors – so-called 'free' publicity – are all important additions to paid-for advertising. Television is generally too expensive as an advertising medium, but book programmes, especially the **Richard and Judy Book Club,** have proved to be very influential in introducing less familiar authors to a wide general readership. In 2007 their fiction choices accounted for 22 per cent of the value of the sales of the top hundred paperbacks and 1.5 per cent of the total consumer market.

Books also seem quite responsive to viral or **word-of-mouth marketing**, and book clubs or reading groups are a good channel for word-of-mouth promotion. There is a wide range of book prizes and awards, some of which – notably the Man Booker prize for fiction – attract television and newspaper coverage and can provide a substantial boost to sales.

Authors' Agents and Rights

Authors' agents have come to play **an increasingly important role** in consumer publishing, and most fiction and many other genres of trade book are acquired by or commissioned through agents. Agents also play an increasing role in providing preliminary editorial advice and shaping projects. Their influence has increased as the range of potential subsidiary rights – audio, video, and electronic – has increased. This has produced some tension between agents and publishers, with the former wanting to separate out as many rights as possible and license them separately, and the publishers, especially the international groups, attempting to acquire control of all language, territorial, and format rights.

The International Trade in Consumer Publishing

Accurate figures on the international sale of rights are hard to establish, although the PA is now undertaking a more comprehensive survey than the one it piloted in 2004. Some estimates suggest that authors and publishers earn in excess of £300m a year in foreign rights and co-edition income. UK publishers generally have well-established networks of partners in foreign markets, but are always on the lookout as new markets open up, as was the case in East and Central Europe in the 1990s, and currently in emerging major markets such as China and India. These activities are frequently focused on the international book fairs, of which there are now dozens around the globe and around the calendar. The **Frankfurt Book Fair** is by far the most important, but the **London Book Fair** (LBF) (www.london-bookfair.co.uk) is now the most important international fair in the spring. Other key fairs for British publishers include Bologna, for children's books, Book Expo America and, increasingly, Beijing and Moscow.

The PA Survey suggests that fiction, adult non-fiction and children's books accounted for 19 per cent, 14 per cent and 21 per cent of UK publishers' invoiced export sales by volume, and 15 per cent, 12 per cent and 25 per cent by value in 2007. These proportions have been fairly stable, with children's publishing gaining several points in value in Harry Potter years.

Europe and Australasia are by far the most important markets for exported fiction , accounting for 39 per cent and 34 percent, non-fiction, accounting for 40 per cent and 18 per cent, and for children's books in a Harry Potter year, accounting for 38 per cent and 22 per cent. The North America is relatively less important export area for consumer books, but UK publishing earns significant amounts from rights and co-edition sales in the region.

The PA estimates that imported book sales at retail value amounted to £57m for fiction, £65m for adult non-fiction and £33m for children's books in 2007.

The Market Environment

Operating as it does in a number of heterogeneous sectors, UK publishing is subject to a complex set of market variables.

The Political Context

While UK publishing, like all other industries, is subject to many governmental and EU laws and regulations, there is **very little direct control** over the industry: any individual or company, British of foreign, can set up as a publisher; there is no form of censorship; educational books are not subject to an approval process, and there are no controls over the pricing of school textbooks or other books.

Books and most other forms of printed matter are **free from VAT** (though not electronic product, on which there is the standard level of tax) despite pressure from time to time from the EC to apply a reduced level of sales tax as is the norm in most EU members. Recent governments, of different political persuasions, have all been committed to raising standards in schools, promoting reading, expanding university education, encouraging connectivity in schools, colleges and homes, and encouraging the export of published products. These have all been indirect positive factors for the UK publishing industry.

As in any other complex developed economy, commerce and industry in the UK are subject to a mass of legislation and regulation. This emanates from local and central government, the European Community, and international bodies such as the World Trade Organisation. However, direct government participation in economic and commercial activity is at a low level.

The case of publishing exemplifies this situation very well. Publishing and bookselling are affected both by general legislation and regulations on issues such as consumer protection and trading standards, price-fixing and monopolistic situations against the public interest, and issues more specific to publishing such as copyright, obscenity and libel.

The obverse of this is that there is very little direct support from government for publishing, although central and local government are important direct or indirect customers for books through educational institutions or libraries. Authors and publishers, especially small literary houses, have been dismayed by the relative lack of support for literature and translation from Arts Council England. In 2007/08 literature received $5.5m and this is due to rise to $6m by 2010/11. However, it should also be recognised that the **devolution of government** in many areas of public life, including the arts and culture, in Scotland, Wales and Northern Ireland has led to **significant funding in those parts of the UK for local authors and local publishing**, both in English and Celtic/Gaelic languages.

There is some support for the export activities of British publishers and the promotion of the English language internationally, especially through the British Council, though here too recent policies seem to be reducing the funding given to the promotion of literature. In general **literature gets much less direct state support** than music, art, dance or drama, and publishing is generally viewed as just another commercial activity that must fend for itself in a competitive market environment.

Governmental Departments

No single government ministry or agency has particular responsibility for the publishing industry, nor is it directed in any way in how it operates commercially. However, the industry does have a number of different relationships with governmental organisations.

Department (Ministry) for Business, Enterprise and Regulatory Reform (www.berr.gov.uk), formerly the Department of Trade and Industry, BERR has, as its name implies, **strategic responsibility** for British industry, and the publishing media and creative industries are recognised as an important part of that accounting for around 7 per cent of GDP. The Department compiles export and import statistics, and carries out or commissions reports on important aspects of industry. In 2002 it published a major study of all forms of printed media entitled *Publishing in the Knowledge Economy: Competitiveness analysis of the UK publishing* *media sector* and a supplementary report, *E-Commerce Opportunities for Publishers*. Both have now been overtaken, to some extent, by events, but still make interesting reading about the strategic issues. They can be accessed on www.berr.gov.uk/sectors/publishing/index.html.

Book publishing emerged well from these surveys as highly competitive in world markets. The Department has so far supported the general government policy of zero-rating printed media for VAT.

UK Trade and Investment (https://uktradeinvest.gov.uk/ukti/appmanager) is the government organisation that provides **advice and some help to exporting companies**. For instance, it has subsidised a number of small and medium companies exhibiting for the first time at the Frankfurt, Bologna, Warsaw, South Africa and Beijing International Book Fairs and at BookExpo America. It has also given some subsidies to overseas trade missions mounted by the PA and to the production of profiles of potential export markets for books.

Department (Ministry) for Children, Schools and Families (www.dcsf.gov.uk), **Department for Innovation, Universities and Skills** (www.dius.gov.uk), formerly the Department for Education and Skills. These Departments are very important as indirect customers for publishing. They disburse funding to schools, colleges and universities, some directly, some indirectly through local authorities and the higher education funding councils. In the case of schools, some of this funding goes to pay for textbooks, which are provided free to pupils, and to school library provision. In colleges and universities funding goes in part to libraries, but students buy their own textbooks. Schools are responsible for their own budgets, and the educational publishers regularly lobby for adequate provision to meet curriculum needs. In recent years the DCFS has made money available for special initiatives in reading and mathematics at primary-school level, but generally the funding allocated to learning resources is regarded as inadequate by teachers and parents.

Department (Ministry) for Culture, Media and Sport (www.dcms.gov.uk). The DCMS has responsibility for all aspects of the nation's culture. It has comparatively limited direct dealings with publishing as an industry, but is has launched an initiative known as the **Creative Economy Programme** (www.cep.culture.gov.uk). This has resulted in a government strategy paper *Creative Britain: New Talents for the New Economy* published in February 2008 (www.culture.gov.uk/Reference_library/Publications/archive_2008/cepPub-new-talents.htm). This is concerned with the development of strategies to encourage the creative industries, including publishing, which are seen as a very successful area of the economy. Indeed, OECD and other organisations have reported that **the UK is the largest exporter of 'cultural**

products' in the world ahead of the USA. Through the Arts Council England (there are separate Arts Councils for Wales, Northern Ireland and Scotland), a limited amount of money is available to subsidise small, specialist publishers, and to help authors and support translations. The Department also has overall responsibility for **public libraries**, though management and funding is applied by local government authorities. The other department involved in this activity is the Department for Communities and Local Government (www.communities.gov.uk).

Foreign and Commonwealth Office (Ministry) (www.fco.gov.uk) **and Department (Ministry) for International Development** (www.dfid.gov.uk). The FCO has overall responsibility for the **British Council** (www.british-council.org) – a semi-autonomous organisation that provides representation of British arts and culture and the English language worldwide. The British Council offices in 240 cities and 110 countries act as the cultural departments of the British high commissions and embassies. They house reading rooms for British books, and many run English-language teaching programmes. They also stage British book exhibitions and author tours, and are very active in the promotion of British authorship internationally. However, there has been recent **concern that the Council is downgrading these latter activities** and withdrawing activities from important markets in Europe and elsewhere to focus on the Middle East and Asia. The British Council also acts as an agent for the Department for International Development (DfID) for many book aid schemes in the developing world.

Official Publishing

Direct government participation in publishing has been **reduced to a minimum**. There was a substantial publishing and minor book retailing operation controlled by the government in the form of **Her Majesty's Stationary Office** (HMSO). HMSO was responsible for the publication of legislation and other official documents, but had also developed as a publisher of general information about the UK, and it had a number of its own bookshops. In 1996 it was privatised and became The Stationery Office. TSO continues to publish many official publications under commission from government departments, producing 15,000 titles a year and offering a wide range of material in P-o-D or online form. There is a residual government operation – the **Office of Public Sector Information** (OPSI) – with responsibility for the publication of certain official documents and the administration of **Crown Copyright** (www.opsi.gov.uk), which is combined with the **National Archives** (www.nationalarchives.gov.uk).

The only other significant government publishing operation is the **Ordnance Survey** (www.ordnancesurvey.co.uk), which is responsible for the official mapping of the UK and publishes directly and under licence an extremely wide range of cartographic materials, both in print and, increasingly, in electronic form.

Publishing and the Law

Legislation that affects publishing may be of a general nature – for instance, laws on consumer protection or more specific to the industry – for instance, copyright law. It may also be protective or enabling (again copyright law), or punitive and restrictive (for instance, laws on defamation and obscenity).

Copyright Law

The formalised protection for the content of printed works is generally dated to the Statute of Anne of 1709, which initially granted exclusive rights to authors for 14 years from the date of publication, renewable once. These rights were progressively extended in terms of the kind of intellectual property covered and the length of time the rights lasted. Today, copyright law in the UK covers all original literary, dramatic, musical or artistic works, sound recordings, films, broadcasts and cable programmes, and typographical arrangements. With some qualifications, it also covers databases, computer programmes, and material on the Internet.

Whether the work exists as ink on paper or is digitally stored, the protection now usually runs for 70 years after the death of the creator. The copyright owner of such works is normally the author (though rights in works created in the course of employment may be owned by the employer). The creator's rights are automatic – the work does not have to be registered – and they can be licensed (often to a publisher in return for a royalty), sold for an outright fee, given away, waived (in the case of moral rights), or bequeathed.

There are different periods of copyright coverage for films, musical recordings and broadcasts. There is also a right in the typographical arrangements of print works, which normally belongs to the publisher and lasts for 25 years from publication, regardless of whether the content is in copyright or not.

In the UK, copyright laws and regulations today stem from a number of sources including UK Acts of Parliament, notably the current **1988**

Copyright, Designs and Patents Act, which introduced the concept of moral rights into UK law. The Act has subsequently been amended in a number of important ways to harmonise UK and EC law, notably by the extension of the term of copyright in printed and many other works to 70 years after the creator's death, in line with an **EC 1995 Directive.** In 2001 the EC produced a further Copyright Directive, concerned especially with issues arising from the challenges of the electronic environment for copyright. This was finally implemented in 2003 in the UK.

The UK was one of the founding members of the Berne Convention (1886), which introduced the practice of multilateral reciprocity in copyright protection among its international membership (now covering 150 countries), and in 1957 joined the Universal Copyright Convention (1952), a slightly less stringent agreement that had been established to accommodate the USA and USSR, which had not acceded to Berne. In 1996 the **World International Copyright Organization** (WIPO) (www.wipo.int) Copyright Treaty brought the Berne agreement up to date for the digital society. In 1994 the **World Trade Organization** (www.wto.org) established the Trade Related Aspects of Intellectual Property (TRIPS) agreement. This committed WTO members to both the principles of Berne and the establishment of effective measures for their enforcement. The UK has signed up to all these international initiatives.

Commercial Rights

The copyright holder of a piece of intellectual property generally has the commercial rights in its exploitation in any form, and these can be sold or licensed as a whole to a single publisher or they can be sub-divided by the author, or more commonly their agent, category by category, with the primary publisher only being licensed with certain volume rights. For a foreign publisher seeking to license rights for a book first published in the UK, the situation can be frustrating since the original book publisher may well not have the translation or other relevant rights, and the author or agent may be hard to track down.

Authors may grant **language rights** in all languages and territories of publication to a publisher – world rights – or divide the rights by language between different publishers.

Even for a single language, **territorial rights** may be granted worldwide – world English-language rights, for instance – or divided by markets. In the case of English, the pattern has been quite frequently to divide English-language rights exclusively to different publishers in the UK and USA and leave the rest of the world open for either party to sell into. This was the case, for instance, with *Harry Potter*, published in English in the UK by Bloomsbury and in the USA by Scholastic. UK-based publishers frequently seek to find ways to exclude American versions from Europe, and are themselves frequently excluded from Canada. How these rights are to be divided is an ongoing source of dispute between British and American publishers, the authors' agents and European booksellers, who may prefer to import cheaper American editions of popular books.

Authors and agents may try to limit the time period or **term** for which a copyright licence runs, but in most cases it continues for the full term of copyright, provided that the publisher keeps the book in print.

In the past it was quite common in the UK for the hardback and paperback rights in a trade book to be licensed to different publishers. With the integration of the big groups this is much less common, but it can still happen when a small publisher gives an author their first break, and may continue to be granted hardback rights even when the paperback rights have gone to one of the large groups. There are other sorts of **volume rights** – for instance, educational reprint rights, large print rights and condensed book rights.

A growing range of **subsidiary rights** has opened up over recent years, from translation rights to spoken word rights, film rights, merchandising rights (especially for children's' books), and **various forms of electronic reproduction rights**. These latter have been **a source of dispute** between authors/agents and publishers since they were frequently not specified in older contracts. There is a natural tension between the two sides, especially with the large international groups, which seek to obtain all rights for global exploitation of a work, and the agents who may seek to slice the rights into numerous separate deals to the author's benefit. For full coverage of both the contractual and trading aspects of rights, see Lynette Owen's *Selling Rights* and Lynette Owen (ed.), *Clark's Publishing Agreements*, cited in Chapter 6.

Moral Rights

While most laws and regulations are concerned with the economic or financial rights of authors and publishers, there are also other important rights usually described as moral rights. In terms of these there is considerable **international variation**. Some countries do not recognise them; in the USA they exist in a very weak form; while some European countries have extensive moral rights that cannot be waived. UK law is somewhere in the middle. It recognises **paternity,** the right of the author to be publicly acknowledged as such; **integrity,** the right of the author not to have their published work altered in a way that could be seen to compromise its quality; **false attribution**, the right not to have work credited to them which is not their own; and **privacy** in relation to some photographic images or films.

In the UK authors must assert the first right, or they may waive the first and second rights. If the author's rights are infringed there is normally recourse through the civil law.

Other Benefits Stemming from Copyright

An important right that exists in the UK, but not all countries, is the **Public Lending Right**, which gives registered authors a modest payment every time their book is borrowed from a public library.

There is also a well-developed system for collecting fees from schools, colleges and businesses that copy limited amounts of copyright material under licence. The operational focus for this work is the **Copyright Licensing Agency** (CLA) (www.cla.co.uk), which is jointly owned by an authors' organisation, the **Authors' Licensing and Collecting Society** (ALCS) (www.alcs.co.uk), and the publishers' equivalent body, the **Publishers Licensing Society** (PLS) (www.pls.org.uk). The CLA also works closely with the **Design and Artists Copyright Society** (www.dacs.org.uk).

ALCS has over 55,000 author members, and distributes over £13m a year to them in collective licensing fees. It works closely with the two other main authors' organisations – the Society of Authors, which has over 8,000 published authors in membership – and the Writers' Guild (www.writers-guild.org.uk), which is a trade union for authors of all kinds, including those working in film, television, radio, theatre and computer games. PLS is jointly owned by the Association of Learned and Professional Society Publishers (www.alpsp.org.uk), the Periodical Publishers Association (www.ppa.co.uk) and The Publishers Association (www.publishers.org.uk). In its last financial year PLS distributed over £20m to publisher rights holders.

Infringement, Piracy and Redress

A great deal of infringement of copyright in print material is inadvertent and of marginal importance in the UK. The main concerns are the illegal copying of copyright material for educational course packs or the importation of copyright material from abroad that infringes the rights of UK rights holders. Unlike in many markets, the substantial illicit reproduction of printed copyright material is extremely rare, and would be treated as a criminal offence with a heavy maximum penalty of ten years imprisonment.

Another form of infringement is **plagiarism**, where one author uses another's material in some way. The most high-profile example of this issue recently was the case brought by two authors against Dan Brown for plagiarism of their work in *The Da Vinci Code*. In that case the claimants lost.

The **situation with DVDs, CDs, audio books, e-books and online material is very different**, and here illicit copying on an amateur level is much more common, and there are also many examples of piracy at a commercial level. A very important recommendation of the 2006 **Gowers Report to the Treasury** (www.hm-treasury.gov.uk/independent_reviews/gowers_review_intellectual_property) on copyright was that penalties for electronic copying of copyright material should match that for physical piracy and that Trading Standards Officers would be funded to track down and prosecute infringers. The report also recommended making civil redress against infringement cheaper.

A quite different range of issues surrounds the question of digital corpuses of material and open access to research. The question of digital banks of content is a contentious one. Governmental bodies, including the EC, with its **European Digital Library project** (www.edlproject.eu) are committed to creating banks of content of the summation of human endeavour, and commercial search engines see a business to be built around the mass digitisation of collections of material, such as the collections of the world's great libraries. Such initiatives when applied to collections of material still in copyright clearly have the potential for infringing authors' and publishers' rights if due permission is not sought, and how to achieve this remains an issue of dispute and potential litigation between the protagonists.

On the issue of international copyright piracy and the infringement of market rights, the PA has taken a leading role, in partnership especially with its American counterpart, in negotiating with governments and pursuing large-scale commercial pirates through the courts in key areas including India, China, Pakistan and Turkey, with some very positive outcomes on both accounts.

Contracts

Author/publisher contracts are governed by general commercial law, and although various 'model' publishing contracts have been devised – notably in *Clark's Publishing Agreements* edited by Lynette Owen (see Part Six) – and are widely used, there is **no specific legislation** to control the relationships between authors and publishers, or the form of contract they agree between themselves.

Restrictive Legislation

As has been noted, there is no form of pre-publication control in British publishing, but book and other publishers must be aware that they may be taken to court to face civil or criminal charges if they infringe the terms of certain pieces of legislation. The most relevant are **defamation and obscenity laws**. Defamation law is concerned with libel – publishing in print damaging and untrue statements about a living individual or group of people. While more likely to occur in newspapers or magazines, it is not unknown in books of modern history, politics, biography, or even novels. This is also true of the developing **privacy legislation** in the UK, which tries to find a fair balance between the rights of the individual and the freedom to publish.

Obscenity is the offence of publishing material that is likely to deprave or corrupt its readers. This is aimed to control blatant pornography, and there is a defence in terms of literary merit. Over recent years the courts have been increasingly permissive, reflecting changing social attitudes.

There is also an offence of Incitement to Racial Hatred – again this is more likely to occur in newspapers and magazines than in books. In 2005 the government also introduced legislation to make it an offence to glorify or encourage acts of terrorism in the spoken or written word.

The Official Secrets Act, which controls the publication of various categories of state information, was significantly liberalised in 1989, and the courts have thrown out a number of prosecutions in recent years. In general, the EC approach to **Freedom of Information** has been adopted, and society expects increasing transparency from government.

General **consumer protection legislation** applies to book publishing. So book buyers have protection against misleading advertisements or the supply of bad quality goods. Book buyers, like other consumers, also have protection against the negative impact of monopolies. If a company comes to control a significant sector of the market for goods or services, it may be referred to the **Office of Fair Trading**, which will investigate whether this dominant position is being used against the interests of the public. If that appears to be the case, the company may be referred to the **Competition Commission**, which can force companies to dilute their market dominance

In 2006, the Competition Commission ruled that the acquisition of Ottakar's, the third largest bookshop chain, by Waterstone's, the largest by value of book sales, did not threaten the public interest because of the competition that would continue to be supplied by W.H.Smith – the second largest chain in terms of book sales, the supermarkets and the e-retailers.

In 2007 the OFT referred the bid for wholesaler Bertrams by Woolworths to the Competition Commission in view of the possibility that it would give Woolworths too dominant a position in the wholesale book market. This was also ruled to be not against the public interest. The purchase of Harcourt Education by Pearson was also approved in 2007.

The Economic Context

Over the last decade the UK economy has generally performed ahead of most of its European Union partners with GDP growth of 3.1 per cent in 2007. Inflation at around 2.1 per cent in terms of the consumer price index was well below the EU figure of 3.1 per cent at the end of 2007. Despite concerns about future economic trends and some turmoil in the financial sector, employment at the end of 2007 was higher than at any time in the last 35 years.

Most people have seen their standard of living improve in recent decades, although there remain a significant number of people below the poverty line. There has been a steady increase in leisure spending (recreation and culture). By 2007 the average weekly family spend reached around £450, of which leisure spending at 14 per cent was the second highest category, only exceeded by transport and ahead of food, beverages and clothing.

Books fall within this recreational category and have benefited from this **extra disposable income**. This has been reflected in a greater willingness amongst readers to buy hardbacks rather than wait for paperback editions and to buy rather than to borrow from libraries. However, consumer publishing has found itself competing in the domestic market with a wide range of other leisure goods and activities. Other sectors of the publishing industry have faced similar challenges. For instance, although there has been some increase in spending on academic and public libraries, this **has not been reflected in book purchases**. The same has been true in schools and colleges; student spending on books has inevitably been affected by the imposition of fees and the increase in student debt.

In common with the rest of British industry, publishing now seems likely to be facing some years of less benign economic conditions, which will impact on both private and public spending. There may be some comfort in the fact that in past periods of recession books seem to have been less vulnerable to cutbacks in personal expenditure than other, more expensive leisure goods and activities.

One downside of the strength of the economy for a high-exporting industry such as publishing has been that the pound sterling has been relatively strong in the foreign exchange markets, especially against the US dollar, its most important single publishing export market and its main competitor in the English language markets worldwide. Recently there has been some weakening of the pound, especially against the Euro, which should be helpful for British book exports, although British publishers may also find themselves faced with higher manufacturing costs in Europe and the Far East.

The Social Context

The population of the UK is predominantly urban, and the majority of those who do live in the countryside have easy access to towns and cities. Given this concentration of population in a small geographical area, and generally effective transport and postal systems, physical book distribution and access to libraries and book-retailing outlets of various kinds is quite straightforward. The same is true of the e-retailing of books, with Amazon usually able to offer a next day delivery on orders.

The overwhelming majority of the population is at least **technically literate in English**. Over 92 per cent of the population define themselves as white Caucasians, but there are significant groups of people whose ethnic origins are in Asia, Africa or the Caribbean, especially in London and other major cities. The UK is **ethnically diverse** as a result of both historical migrations and more recent newcomers, including most recently long- and short-term migrants from elsewhere in the EU. There is a very small natural population growth enhanced by net immigration of over 200,000 a year. Nevertheless, the population is ageing, and although older people are better off than they were in previous generations, this situation may be hard to sustain with a decline of the proportion of the population in employment.

English is overwhelmingly the most commonly used language, with the only other substantial indigenous language being **Welsh**, which is spoken as a first language by over 500,000 people. It is government policy to require new immigrants to learn English before they arrive, or to take compulsory classes when they take up residence. Nevertheless, the UK demonstrates considerable **cultural diversity**, both between its constituent parts and within them. One interesting outcome of the migration of considerable numbers of people from Eastern Europe to the UK has been the retailing of titles in other European languages, notably Mills and Boon romances in Polish.

The recent years of comparative economic success have produced **a prosperous, leisured society by world standards**, with high levels of home ownership, possession of a diverse range of consumer goods, and wide experience of foreign travel. These social factors all have an impact on the publishing industries, mainly in positive ways.

The UK has **high general levels of literacy** and books are read in most households. Women and girls read more books than men and boys, and the lowest levels of book reading are found among teenage boys. **The heaviest readers**, in terms of time spent in the activity, are women of 16–19 years and over 55 years. There are differences also in genres, with girls and women reading fiction much more heavily than men and boys, although the latter are more likely to be readers of particular fiction genres such as science fiction and fantasy. Men also read more history, sport and practical books. **Reading as a leisure activity has grown steadily** over the last 20 years, along with listening to music, while television viewing has remained quite static, or this 'screen time' time has been transferred from this activity to going online on a computer.

Book buying, however, has been remarkably resilient in the face of competition from alternative forms of information and entertainment. Since 1999 the absolute amount spent on books by consumers has increased alongside the general level of leisure spending. However, it has remained steady as a proportion (3–4 per cent of leisure spending), and while half the population buys some books, **80 per cent of purchases come from the top 20 per cent of book buyers**. Overall, 37 per cent of people claim they buy at least one book a month – 43 per cent of women and 31 per cent of men. On the other hand a quarter of the population say they never buy books.

In the UK consumer book market **women were responsible for 59 per cent of purchases by volume and 52 per cent by value** although men accounted for rather more of the growth in the year. Women tend to be the main buyers of **books as gifts** for both their own family members and others and the buying of books as gifts has increased by 25% by volume and 17 per cent by value over the last four years.

BML's figures suggest that growth in book purchases in 2007 came mainly from 35–54 and 55–79 year-olds, while sales to younger people declined. Over the last four years the greatest growth has come in the 55–79 year old group. However, this older generation may not be so prosperous in the future. They also indicate that growth in recent years has mainly come from socio-economic groups C, D and E although proportionately As and Bs are the heaviest buyers, suggesting that the upper end of the market is fairly mature, but there is room for growth at the lower end.

The Reading Agency and BML surveyed reading habits and library use in 2005 and concluded that 74 per cent of all adults read some books, with 69 per cent of men and 78 per cent of women reading. Women read more than men in all categories, but especially fiction where 59 per cent of readers were women. In terms of socio-economic class 88 per cent of A/Bs were readers as opposed to 60 per cent of D/Es while the over 35 year-olds read significantly more than younger adults.

In 2005 the government considerably extended its encouragement of literacy and a love of books by putting some £27m into the **Book Start** programme (www.bookstart.org.uk), a scheme under which all young children are given a pack of suitable books (and writing materials for older children) in their first, second and third years. Booktouch is an extension of the scheme for blind and visually impaired children. Government funding is now available for two further schemes: **Booktime** (www.booktime.pearson.com) aimed at early primary school classes and **Booked Up** (www.bookedup.org.uk), which aims to provide every Year 7 pupil in England with a book.

A National Foundation for Educational Research Survey in 2007 suggests that reading remains as popular as ever amongst pre-teen children, though not necessarily in traditional book format. *The Bookseller* magazine is currently launching its own survey of reading habits in the UK.

The Technological Context

All aspects of life in general, and the UK media and publishing industries in particular, are being transformed by the impact of technology. The country has one of the highest levels of Internet connectivity in Europe, with 61 per cent of households and the great majority of businesses and all educational institutions able to access the Internet. Over 84 per cent of household Internet connections are now made via broadband. **Over two-thirds of the population are Internet users** compared with an EC average of 55 per cent.

People in the UK are the highest users of e-shopping (including book purchase) in any of the major European markets, and have tended to be early adopters of new technology facilities such as advanced mobile phones and iPods. In business **e-commerce** is increasingly widely used, and the target for adoption throughout the book trade is May 2008. Penetration of mobile phones is currently running at 105 per cent, and the UK has one of the highest levels of digital television penetration in Europe.

The UK also has some of **the highest levels of information and communications technology (ICT) in all stages of education** in

Europe, and the government has encouraged heavy investment in hardware and software in schools, colleges and public and educational libraries.

This availability of a range of digital technologies in all areas of life can be seen as both a threat and an opportunity for publishers, depending on how they chose to engage with them.

The application of digital technology to publishing processes really began in book distribution with the decision of the country's largest book retailer, W.H.Smith, to computerise its warehouse in 1966. This led directly to the creation of the Standard Book Number (SBN) system, which was rapidly applied to almost all book publications in the UK, and was extended into **an international system (ISBN) in 1970**. The system of giving a unique 11-digit identifying number to every publication was to become fundamental to the subsequent development of modern systems of book distribution, bibliography, sales data and e-commerce. In 2007, with the explosion of new titles worldwide, the 11 digits became 13.

Digital technology progressively began to transform text origination and editing, the capture and storage of images, and printing processes. It allowed for the instantaneous transfer of text and image to multiple sites for local printing, and the development of print-on-demand. It has become the basis for many modern direct marketing systems and allowed publishers and booksellers to undertake sophisticated sales and marketing analyses.

Not only publishing processes, but also products were soon affected by the so-called 'new technology'. Here progress was less seamless, with publishers going up a number of (sometimes very expensive) dead ends. In the early 1980s many publishers experimented with software for **the first small home computers**, but there were major problems with incompatibility between different types of hardware, a lack of market understanding of what consumers really wanted, and an uncertainty about the appropriate channels of distribution. Publisher interest fizzled out, and the market was more or less abandoned to the computer games companies.

In the 1990s consumer CDs were to prove an even more expensive area of experiment with a transitory technology for a number of publishers, and the early electronic book-reading devices never achieved lift-off with the public. In general, the process of transfer from ink-on-paper to electronic delivery of book product was much slower than the industry gurus predicted in the early 1990s. As late as 1996 Andersen Consulting were predicting in a report for the EC that 5 per cent of European trade publishing, 15 per cent of STM, and 15 per cent of business-to-business publishing would be electronic by 2000. Even these quite modest levels were premature. However, the report was correct in suggesting that **STM** and business publishing would advance into an electronic environment most rapidly, and by 2008 electronic had become the predominant mode of delivery in some sectors, such as scientific journals and legal, medical and regulatory databases.

For consumer publishing, partial conversion to electronic delivery was under way, though there was still only a tentative understanding of which types of content and which modes of distribution would ultimately prove to be financially viable in this new publishing environment. In the continuum from author to reader new roles were still to be defined for all parties, including publishers, booksellers and librarians, and **major questions concerning the status and security of IP await resolution.**

So far as **e-retailing** is concerned, books remain one of the most popular Internet purchases, along with DVDs, airline tickets, music and clothing. In terms of e-shopping as a whole, e-Bay UK leads with around 40 per cent, followed by Amazon UK with 10 per cent of the market, ahead of Argos, Tesco, and Marks and Spencer. For books, Amazon is far and away the market leader, as can be seen from the table below. However, by far the most popular book-related site is Google Book Search, which explains the concern that publishers have about their copyright materials being freely accessible in part or in whole

● **Top Ten UK Book and Magazine e-Retailers by Market Share, 2006**

Retailer	Market Share %
1 Amazon UK	70.2
2 Amazon US	11.5
3 W.H.Smith	1.6
4 Abebooks UK	1.3
5 E-Bay UK	1.1
6 Amazon Japan	1.0
7 Abebooks US	1.0
8 Waterstone's	0.7
9 Tesco Books	0.7
10 The Book People	0.7

Source: Hitwise, www.hitwise.co.uk

Text, Books and Publishers in the 21st Century

At a time of seismic change, both commercial and technological, predictions are notoriously hard to make and looking back over the last twenty years it is interesting to see how wrong the gurus were about how book publishing would change in terms of both velocity and market specifics. But they were much less wrong about the general direction of change. Today publishers can take some comfort from some remarkably stable elements in a market environment subject to accelerating change, always conscious of the fact that the past, even the immediate past, is not necessarily a good guide to the future.

The Primacy of Text

One aspect of the current publishing environment that was not altogether anticipated is the continuing primacy of text. Today online searching, blogs, social network sites, e-mailing and texting involve more people than ever in more and more writing and reading, partially, for better or worse, at the expense of oral communication. However, the act of delivering and receiving text is being transformed and this is all part of an historical continuum. Writing in one form or another is now in its fifth millennium, but in Europe it was only in the fourteenth century that reading silently or without moving your lips became general practice and it was around that time that the modern conventions of punctuation, inverted commas for speech, paragraphing and so on became established.

Likewise today we are going through a similar period of significant change. Reading a book is usually a thoughtful, linear, vertical process. Reading and researching on-line, as much recent research has shown, is thought provoking, 'bouncing' and non-sequential. The implication for publishers is that for at least part of their market they need to rethink how content is designed and organised to meet the needs of new users – 'the Google generation'. Recent research shows that 89 per cent of students begin their information searches with a search engine as opposed to searching a library database. The very latest research suggests these profound shifts in information-seeking behaviours are not confined to the young and that 'information literacy' will need to be redefined. At the same time there is a lack of firm evidence of how many downloads are actually read, as opposed to squirreled away. The primacy of text as a means of communication remains, but publishers and authors are still **coming to terms with what the new ways of reading will be in different genres.**

The Resilience of the Book

The codex or hinged book long pre-dates the Gutenberg revolution, going back to the second century AD, but its high point as a mass cultural product followed from the invention of printing with moveable type in the West in the 15th century and the invention of steam-powered printing in the 19th century. Subsequent technological advances in origination and production have immensely improved the affordability, quality and diversity of the product, but not essentially changed its nature.

The predictions of **the imminent death of the book** from the 1980s onwards were clearly misplaced or at least mistimed. In certain sectors of publishing delivery of content by other means has now become the norm, but globally, as in the UK, the output of printed books by volume and in terms of numbers of new titles has grown inexorably in recent decades. Books have retained their status as highly desirable possessions in the consumer markets of the West or the book-starved educational markets of the developing world. It seems that people's relationship with the book as a physical object goes beyond purely utilitarian considerations.

A recent survey of 26,000 Internet users in 46 countries carried out by Nielsen Online suggested that 40 per cent of online shoppers worldwide bought books, the top product ahead of clothing, travel and music. Some of the highest levels of book purchase were in emerging markets such as China, Brazil and Egypt, but **books were also the number one product in the UK with 45 per cent of online shoppers buying them**.

However, there are also some contra indications. In China, now the largest book market in the world by volume and second largest by value in purchasing power parity terms, a high proportion of the very lively youth literature genre is now published predominantly online – and frequently **consumed on mobile phones** on crowded commuter trains. It is also worth remembering that for eighty years after the Gutenberg revolution the production of hand-scribed books actually increased in Europe, before rapidly collapsing. Today the tipping-points of technological change are likely to come much more quickly – but in the case of the book **the iPod moment** seems to be not now and probably not for some time in many publishing sectors.

The Enduring Role of the Publisher

The premature discussions of the death of the book often also assumed the death of the publisher. Such thinking failed to recognise that **the essential publishing functions are not dependent on one particular means of delivering intellectual content**. To under this point, one has only to look at the way in which Reed Elsevier or Thomson have transformed themselves from traditional publishers into highly profitably electronic content deliverers, because their chosen market sector required it.

Publishing is first and foremost an entrepreneurial, risk-taking business, with publishers selecting product and funding authorship, product development, marketing and delivery. Successful publishers provide authentication and quality assurance to the ultimate consumer. They also have, in many forms of publishing, a highly creative role, perceiving market needs and commissioning the product to meet them. Even in author-led sectors, such as literature, there are endless examples of successful books which have resulted from the symbiotic relationship between author and editor. All these roles and skills are needed in publishing whatever the medium and whatever the structure of the industry.

In the recent past there was much discussion of **the impact of 'disintermediation' on publishers**, that is to say the sidelining of publishers as a result of the direct relationship the author and the readership can have in an electronic environment. Such thinking largely ignored the added value that the publishers brought to the shaping of the final product and to the distribution chain, electronic or physical. In practice it now seems that electronic delivery brings the publisher into much more direct and personalised contact with the ultimate consumer and it is more likely that the bookseller and librarian may find their intermediary roles diminished.

The Publishers Association and Publishing-Related Organisations

The Publishers Association

The first effective modern publishing organisation in the UK was The Publishers Association, founded in 1896 by the leading publishers of the day to bring some order to the book trade in collaboration with the recently formed Booksellers Association. They remain the two key organisations for the self-regulation and promotion of book publishing and distribution. Almost all booksellers, including the chains, some supermarkets and the independents belong to the Booksellers Association (it has 3,200 members). Around 180 publishers belong to The Publishers Association out of 2,200 publishing companies of any significance. In practice, the PA members account for over 80 per cent of the UK book business by value and the Association is recognised by government and the trade as a whole as the public voice of the book publishing industry.

The Publishers Association is a not-for-profit, private organisation. It is funded by membership fees, calculated in proportion to the sales revenue of members, and its membership includes almost all the major commercial book-publishing groups and many important smaller publishers. The Publishers Association caters for all sectors of book and electronic publishing through its divisions, which provide sector-specific services and expertise. A complete list of PA members is available at www.publishers.org.uk.

The Publishers Association has a governing Council, elected by the membership, and a President and Vice-President/Treasurer who are elected from the membership to serve for a year at a time. The permanent staff includes a Chief Executive, Director of International and Trade Services and Director of Educational, Academic and Professional Publishing along with specialist managers and advisers on such matters as Statistics, Copyright, and Book Fairs.

The Publishers Association is the focal point where publishers come together to identify and discuss the main issues facing their industry and where the policies are developed that drive the PA's campaigns to ensure a secure trading environment for the industry. At the heart of its work is negotiation with the UK government and with the EC on issues affecting the market, sometimes on its own and sometimes in alliance with other groups such as UK Publishing Media (www.ukpublishingmedia.org), which includes the trade associations for newspapers and magazines, or the Federation of European Publishers (www.fep-fee.org). It makes regular submissions to government and EC consultations on issues such as copyright, scientific publications and the creative economy.

The International Division actively supports the international sales activities of PA members, to improve performance in sales and rights business worldwide. It also leads the international campaign against book piracy. It has subsidiary working parties that focus on key export regions.

The Academic and Professional Division brings together publishers of college, university, academic and professional books and journals. It campaigns for the value of textbooks, sustainable funding flows for scholarly journals, respect for copyright in all media, and a collaborative approach to realising opportunities in a digital marketplace. It is also heavily involved in the debate about access to research outputs with research funders, library organisations and the EC.

The Educational Publishers Council represents publishers of learning resources for schools and school library books. It campaigns vigorously for proper financial provision and liaises closely with the agencies of government over matters such as the National Strategies for primary and secondary education and the reform of the 11–19 curriculum

The Trade Publishers Council serves publishers of both fiction and non-fiction. It is concerned with the consumer market, and with the promotion of reading and a book culture.

Membership of the Association brings access to working groups that deal with specialist market sectors, such as children's publishing, legal publishing, religious books and scholarly journals. The PA offers information to members through its website and regular newsletters, as well as conferences and seminars. Working with a network of consultants and advisors, the PA provides information on relevant developments in copyright, publishing law, finance, taxation, employment and environmental legislation. It also provides a range of market statistics, notably through its running survey of the UK market published in its series of *Statistics Yearbooks*.

Market development is also at the heart of many PA activities including national representation at the major book trade fairs around the world and international market intelligence, notably through its Global Publishing Information series.

The Association also represents UK publishing on international bodies such as the International Publishers Association and the Federation of European Publishers, and on joint UK industry and international bodies concerned with issues such as intellectual property and industry supply chain systems, such as Book Industry Communication (BIC).

Full details of the PA's organisation and activities are available on the website, www.publishers.org.uk. Contact details for other publishing and trade organisations are listed below.

Directory of Publishing Addresses

There are a number of other voluntary bodies for publishers, including the Independent Publishers Guild (currently with over 500 members, largely from the smaller publishing companies), and specialist associations in sectors such as audio and online publishing. There are regional bodies in Wales and Scotland, and a variety of associations for individuals as opposed to companies, such as the Society for Editors and Proofreaders, Women in Publishing, and the Society of Young Publishers.

The publishing business is largely self-regulating and depends upon the collaboration of organisations and companies to improve its collective performance. A good example of this is BIC (Book Industry Communication) – a body supported by publishing, bookselling and library organisations to standardise and enhance supply chain dynamics both in the UK and internationally

All addresses are in the United Kingdom unless otherwise noted. If telephoning from abroad to the UK add the country code +44 and omit the first 0 from the number. This list covers organisations mentioned in the text; for a fuller list of relevant bodies and addresses and background on their areas of activity consult the Continuum & The Publishers Association *Directory of Publishing 2008*.

Publishing Organisations

Association of Learned and Professional Society Publishers (ALPSP)
Ian Russell, Chief Executive
Tel: 01275 856 444
Fax: 08707 060 332
Ian.Russell@alpsp.org.uk
www.alpsp.org.uk

Association of Authors' Agents
Penny Holroyde, Secretary
Caroline Sheldon Agency
70-75 Cowcross Street
London EC1M 6EJ
Tel: 020 7336 6550
aaa@carolinesheldon.co.uk
www.agentsassoc.co.uk

Audiobook Publishing Association
Charlotte McCandish, Administrator
Tel: 07971 280788
info@theapa.net
www.theapa.net

Data Publishers Association
Jerry Gosney, Executive Director
Queens House, 28 Kingsway
London WC2B 6JR
Telephone: 020 7405 0836
Fax: 020 7404 4167
info@dpa.org.uk
www.dpa.org.uk

Federation of European Publishers (FEP/FEE)
Anne Bergman-Tahon, Director
Rue Montoyer 31 Bte 8
B-1000 Brussels
Belgium
Tel: +32 2 770 1110
Fax: +32 2 771 2071
abergman@fep-fee.be
www.fep-fee.be

Independent Publishers Guild (IPG)
Bridget Shine, Executive Director
PO Box 93
Royston SG8 5GH
Tel: 01763 247014
Fax: 01763 246293
info@ipg.uk.com
www.ipg.org.uk

International Publishers Association (IPA)
Jens Bammel, Secretary General
3, avenue de Miremont
1206 Geneva
Switzerland
Tel: +41 22 346 3018
Fax: +41 22 347 5717
secretariat@ipa-uie.org
www.ipa-uie.org

International Association of STM Publishers (STM)
Michael Mabe, CEO
2nd Floor, Prama House
267 Banbury Road, Oxford OX2 7HT
Tel: 01865 339 321
Fax: 01865 339 325
mabe@stm-assoc.org
www.stm-assoc.org

London Book Fair
Emma House,
Exhibition Manager – International Development
Reed Exhibitions Ltd
28 The Quadrant, Richmond
Surrey TW9 1DN
Tel: 020 8910 7194
Fax: 020 8910 7930
Emma.House@reedexpo.co.uk
www.londonbookfair.co.uk

Music Publishers Association
Stephen Navin, CEO
6th Floor, British Music House
26 Berners Street, London W1T 3LR
Tel: 020 7580 0126
Fax: 020 7637 3929
info@mpaonline.org.uk
www.mpaonline.org.uk

Periodical Publishers Association
Jonathan Shephard, CEO
(from 1 April 2008)
Queens House, 28 Kingsway
London WC2B 6JR
Tel: 020 7404 4166
Fax: 020 7404 4167
info@ppa.org.uk
www.ppa.org.uk

The Publishers Association
Simon Juden, Chief Executive
29b Montague Street
London WC1B 5BW
Tel: 020 7691 9191
Fax: 020 7691 9199
mail@publishers.org.uk
www.publishers.org.uk

Publishing Scotland (Scottish Publishers Asociation)
Lorraine Fannin, Director (until July 2008)
Scottish Book Centre, 137 Dundee Street
Edinburgh   EH11 1BG
Tel: 0131 228 6866
Fax:0131 228 3220
info@scottishbooks.org
www.scottishbooks.org

Society for Editors and Proofreaders
Riverbank House,
1 Putney Bridge Approach
London SW6 3JD
Tel: 020 7736 3278
Fax: 020 7736 3318
administration@sfep.org.uk
www.sfep.org.uk

Society of Young Publishers
c/o The Bookseller*
Endeavour House,
189 Shaftesbury Avenue
London WC2H 8TJ
sypchair@thesyp.org.uk
www.thesyp.org.uk

UK Association of Online Publishers
Ruth Brownlee, Director
Queens House, 28 Kingsway
London WC2B 6JR
Tel: 020 7404 4166
Fax: 020 7404 4167
info@ukaop.org.uk
www.ukaop.org.uk

Welsh Books Council
Gwerfyl Pierce Jones, Director
Castell Brychan
Aberystwyth
Ceredigion, SY23 2JB
Tel: 01970 624151
Fax: 01970 625385
castellbrychan@wbc.org.uk
www.cllc.org.uk

Women in Publishing
Susan Gunasekera, Membership Secretary
17 Leigh Street
London WC1H 9EW
info@wipub.org.uk
http://wipub.org.uk

Bookselling and Distribution Organisations

The Booksellers Association (www.booksellers.org.uk) is the oldest book trade body in the UK, dating back to 1895. Unusually it draws its membership from two countries – the UK and the Republic of Ireland. It is also very inclusive: its membership covers most independent booksellers in the two markets, all the chains, and a number of other major bookselling outlets, such as the supermarkets. It represents over 4,000 retail outlets selling new books in the two countries.

The BA has been at the front end of trade innovation, from the Book Tokens, which has been running for 75 years, to supply chain systems such as batch.co.uk and it has a lead role in World Book Day. It issues, in association with Nielsen BookData, a definitive guide to book publishers and distributors, and has its own directory of booksellers. The BA has played a leading role in the establishment of new electronic standards in the book trade through BIC, and is a leading member of the European Booksellers Federation. The BA conference, held in various locations in May each year, is the prime meeting point for booksellers and publishers for both professional and social dialogue. The BA's website is very rich in terms of publishing and bookselling-related data, and information on legislation and book trade systems and practice.

There are a number of other book trade organisations with informative websites.

Association of Subscription Agents
Rollo Turner, Secretary General
10 Lime Avenue, High Wycombe
Bucks. HP11 1DP
Tel: 01494 534778
Fax: 01494 534778
rollo.turner@dsl.pipex.com
www.subscription-agents.org

The Booksellers Association of the United Kingdom and Ireland
Tim Godfray, CEO
Minster House, 272 Vauxhall Bridge Road,
London SW1V 1BA
Tel: 020 7802 0802.
Fax: 020 7802 0803.
mail@booksellers.org.uk
www.booksellers.org.uk

British Educational Suppliers Association
Dominic Savage, Director General
20 Beaufort Court, Admirals Way
London E14 9XL
Tel: 020 7537 4997
Fax: 020 7537 4846
Email: besa@besa.org.uk
www.besanet.org

European Booksellers Federation
Francoise Dubruille, Director
Chaussée de Charleroi, 51b, Boite 1
B-1060 Brussels, Belgium
Tel: +32 2 223 49 40
Fax: +32 2 223 49 38
frandubruille.eurobooks@skynet.be
www.ebf-eu.org

International Booksellers Federation
Françoise Dubruille, Director
Chaussée de Charleroi, 51b Boite 1
B-1060 Brussels, Belgium
Tel: +32 2 223 49 40
Fax: +32 2 223 49 38
ibf.booksellers@skynet.be
www.ibf-booksellers.org/newsite

Authors' Organisations, Copyright Organisations and Collecting Societies

Authors' Licensing and Collecting Society
Owen Atkinson, CEO
The Writers' House, 13 Haydon Street
London, EC3N 1DB
Tel: 020 7264 5700
Fax: 020 7264 5755
alcs@alcs.co.uk
www.alcs.co.uk

The Copyright Licensing Agency
Kevin Fitzgerald, CEO
Saffron House, 6-10 Kirby Street
London EC1N 8TS
Tel: 020 7400 3100
Fax: 020 7400 3101
cla@cla.co.uk
www.cla.co.uk

Design and Artists Copyright Society
Joanna Cave, CEO
33 Great Sutton Street
London EC1V 0DX
Tel: 020 7336 8811
Fax: 020 7336 8822
info@dacs.org.uk
www.dacs.org.uk

Publishers Licensing Society
Alicia Wise, CEO
37-41 Gower Street
London WC1E 6HH
Tel: 020 7299 7730
Fax: 020 7299 7780
pls@pls.org.uk
www.pls.org.uk

Society of Authors
Mark Le Fanu, General Secretary
84 Drayton Gardens
London SW10 9SB
Tel: 020 7373 6642
Fax: 020 7373 5768
info@societyofauthors.com
www.societyofauthors.net

World Intellectual Property Organization
34, chemin des Colombettes
PO Box 18, CH-1211 Geneva 20
Switzerland
Tel: +41 22 338 9111
Fax: +41 22 733 5428
www.wipo.int

World Trade Organization
Centre William Rappard, rue de Lausanne 154,
CH-1211 Geneva 21,
Switzerland
Tel: +41 22 739 51 11
Fax: +41 22 731 42 06
enquiries@wto.org
www.wto.org

Writers' Guild of Great Britain
Bernie Corbett, General Secretary
15 Britannia Street
London WC1X 9JN
Tel: 020 7833 0777
Fax: 020 7833 4777
admin@writersguild.org.uk
www.writersguild.org.uk

Library and Bibliographic Organisations

Book Industry Communication (BIC)
39-41 North Road
London N7 9DP
Tel: 020 7607 0021
Fax: 020 7607 0415
info@bic.org.uk
www.bic.org.uk

British Library
96 Euston Road
London NW1 2DB
Tel: 0870 444 1500
info@bl.uk
www.bl.uk

Chartered Institute of Librarians and Information Professionals (CILIP)
7 Ridgmount Street
London WC1E 7AE
Tel: 020 7255 0500
Fax: 020 7255 0501
info@cilip.org.uk
www.cilip.org.uk

Library Information and Statistics Unit (LISU)
Holywell Park
Loughborough University
LE11 3TU
Tel: 01509 63 5680
Fax: 01509 63 5699
lisu@lboro.ac.uk
www.lisu.ac.uk

Nielsen BookData
3rd Floor, Midas House, 62 Goldsworth Road
Woking, Surrey GU21 6LQ
Tel: 0870 777 8710
Fax: 0870 777 8711
sales@nielsenbookdata.co.uk
www.nielsenbookdata.co.uk

School Library Association
Unit 2, Lotmead Business Village, Wanborough
Swindon SN4 0UY
Tel: 08707 770979
Fax: 08707 770987
info@sla.org.uk
www.sla.org.uk

Market Information Providers

Book Marketing Ltd (BML)
7 John Street
London WC1N 2ES
Tel: 020 7440 8930
Fax: 020 7242 7485
bml@bookmarketing.co.uk
www.bookmarketing.co.uk

Nielsen BookScan
3rd Floor, Midas House,
62 Goldsworth Road
Woking, Surrey GU21 6LQ
Tel: 01483 712222
Fax: 01483 712220
info@nielsenbookscan.co.uk
www.nielsenbookscan.co.uk

Outsell
7-15 Rosebery Avenue
London EC1R 4SP
Tel: 020 7837 3345
Fax: 020 7837 8901
www.outsellinc.com

The Publishers Association
29b Montague Street
London WC1B 5BW
Tel: 020 7691 9191
Fax: 020 7691 9199
mail@publishers.org.uk
www.publishers.org.uk

VISTA
Link House
19 Colonial Way, Watford
Hertfordshire WD24 4JL
Tel: 01923 830 200
Fax: 01923 238 789
mjp@vistacomp.com
www.vistacomp.com

Literacy and Reading Organisations

Booktrust
45 East Hill
London SW18 2QZ
Tel:020 8516 2977
Fax 020 8516 2978
query@booktrust.org.uk
www.booktrust.org.uk

National Literacy Trust
Swire House, 59 Buckingham Gate
London SW1E 6AJ
Tel: 020 7828 2435
Fax: 020 7931 9986
contact@literacytrust.org.uk
www.literacytrust.org.uk

The Reading Agency
PO Box 96
St. Albans AL1 3WP
Tel: 0871 750 1207
info@readingagency.org.uk
www.readingagency.org.uk

Scottish Book Trust
Sandeman House, Trunk's Close
55 High Street,
Edinburgh EH1 1SR
Tel: 0131 524 0160
Fax: 0131 524 0161
info@scottishbooktrust.com
www.scottishbooktrust.com

Websites of Government Departments and Agencies Relevant to Publishing

Arts Council England
www.artscouncil.org.uk

Arts Council of Northern Ireland
www.artscouncil-ni.org.uk

**Arts Council Scotland/
Scottish Arts Council**
www.scottisharts.org.uk

Arts Council of Wales
www.artswales.org.uk

British Council
www.britishcouncil.org.uk

**British Educational Communication
Technology Agency**
www.becta.org.uk

Curriculum Online
www.curriculumonline.gov.uk

**Department for Business,
Enterprise and Regulatory Reform**
www.berr.gov.uk

**Department for Children, Schools
and Families**
www.dcsf.gov.uk

**Department for Communities and
Local Government**
www.communities.gov.uk

Department for Culture, Media and Sport
www.dcms.gov.uk

Department for Education Northern Ireland
www.deni.gov.uk

Department for Education and Training in Wales
www.wales.gov.uk

Department for Innovation, Universities and Skills
www.dius.gov.uk

Department for International Development
www.dfid.gov.uk

Foreign and Commonwealth Office
www.fco.gov.uk

Higher Education Research Opportunities in the UK (HERO)
www.hero.ac.uk

Higher Education Statistics Agency (HESA)
www.hesa.ac.uk

Joint Information Systems Committee (JISC)
www.jisc.ac.uk

Museums, Libraries and Archives Council
www.mla.gov.uk

National Archives
www.nationalarchives.gov.uk

Office of Public Sector Information
www.opsi.gov.uk

Office of National Statistics
www.statistics.gov.uk

Ordnance Survey
www.ordnancesurvey.co.uk

Research Information Network
www.rin.ac.uk

Scottish Education and Employment Department
www.scotland.gov.uk

Publishing Education, Training and Recruitment Organisations

London College of Communications
www.lcc.arts.ac.uk

Oxford International Centre for Publishing Studies, Oxford Brookes University
www.brookes.ac.uk

There are a number of other university courses in England and Scotland at University College (London), City (London), Middlesex (London), Luton, Plymouth, Loughborough, Napier (Edinburgh), Nottingham Trent, Stirling and Robert Gordon (Aberdeen).

Publishing Training Centre
www.train4publishing.co.uk

Jobs are advertised in the *Bookseller*, *Publishing News* and the Media Supplement (Mondays) of the *Guardian*. There are also a number of specialist recruitment agencies, including Inspired Selection (London and Oxford), www.inspiredselection.co.uk, Meridian Search and Selection (London), www.meridian-recruit.com, Judy Farquharson/JFL Search and Selection (London), www.jflrecruit.com and Judy Fisher (London), www.JudyFisher.co.uk

Further Reading

This is a selective list of UK publishing reference and professional books
and journals. A much fuller bibliography can be found in Clark, G. *Inside
Book Publishing*, Routledge and at www.insidebookpublishing.com.

Directories and Reference Books

*Directory of Publishing, United Kingdom and the Republic of Ireland
2008*, Continuum and The Publishers Association. This annual publication gives listings of all significant UK publishers and indicates their area
of publishing, key personnel etc. It also lists agents, distributors and
many other publishing industry suppliers and organisations

Directory of UK and Irish Publishers, 2007, The Booksellers Association
and Nielsen BookData. A print and searchable online resource covering
over 6,000 publishers, wholesalers, distributors, sales and marketing
agents and remainder dealers

Directory of UK and Irish Booksellers, 2007, The Booksellers Association

Writers and Artists Handbook, A&C Black. An annual publication; lists
publishers and agents and gives summary information on issues such as
copyright law

The Guardian Media Guide, Guardian Books. An annual directory to all
aspects of the media. Especially useful for addresses of newspapers and
magazines and on the broadcast media

Reports

United Kingdom Publishing Market Profile, The Publishers Association, 2007

The Publishers Association Annual Report, The Publishers Association, 2008

UK Book Publishing Industry Statistics Yearbook 2007, The Publishers Association, 2008

Publishing in the Knowledge Economy, Department of Trade and Industry, 2002

Books and the Consumer, BML, annual

People in Publishing, The Bookseller Publications, 2004

Who Owns Whom in British Publishing, The Bookseller Publications, 2002

From Kitchen Table to Laptop, Independent Publishing in England, Arts Council England, 2005

Publishing Industry Market Review, May 2006, Key Note Ltd

Bookselling Market Report, March 2007, Key Note Ltd

History and Introduction to the Industry

Feather, J., *A History of British Publishing*, Routledge, 1991

Clark, G., *Inside Book Publishing*, Routledge, 2002

de Bellaigue, E., *British Publishing as a Business Since the 1960s*, British Library, 2004

Thompson, J., *Books in the Digital Age*, Polity Press, 2005

Copyright, Contracts and Legal Issues

Jones, H. and Benson, C., *Publishing Law*, Routledge, 2006

Owen, Lynette, (ed.), *Clark's Publishing Agreements*, Tottel, 2007

Owen, Lynette, *Selling Rights*, Routledge, 2006

Electronic Publishing

Bennett, Linda, *e-Books: the Options – a manual for publishers*, The Publishers Association, 2006

e-Commerce

How to get the best out of bookshop systems and e-commerce, Book Industry Communication, 2008 (www.bic.org.uk/e4books/ecommerce-resources.html)

Trade Journals

The Bookseller, a weekly magazine with special spring and autumn supplements featuring forthcoming publications. It has a mixture of news items, articles, and data, including detailed bestseller listings, and job advertisements, www.thebookseller.com.

Publishing News, a weekly newspaper with news, gossip and job advertisements, www.publishingnews.co.uk.

Scholarly Communications Report, a monthly with news and updates on issues impacting the journals market, www.scrpublishing.com.

Information World Review, a monthly update for information professionals with news and forward looking articles on e-books, the web and scholarly publishing, www.iwr.co.uk.

Lightning Source UK Ltd.
Milton Keynes UK
17 August 2009

142733UK00001BA/4/P